Singles Prepare!
Before You Say "I Do"

Pastors Frank & JoeNell Summerfield

ARMOUR OF LIGHT
PUBLISHING

Chapel Hill, North Carolina · Charleston, South Carolina

You can contact the author at:

Summerfield Ministries
PO Box 46891
Raleigh, NC 27620
phone: 919-834-1141
www.summerfieldministries.org

Copyright © 2009 by Pastors Frank & JoeNell Summerfield

Published in the United States of America by
Armour of Light Publishing
P.O. Box 778
Chapel Hill, North Carolina 27514

Visit us at: www.armouroflight.org

Cover Design by Ed Moe for Summerfield Ministries

ISBN 978-0-9825476-0-1

Library of Congress Control Number: 2009909176

First Edition

All scriptures quoted from the Authorized King James Version unless otherwise noted.

10 9 8 7 6 5 4 3 2 *1*

Dedication

A special dedication and thanks to our precious children, Frank Jr., Mitchell, Valisha, and Joshua, all of whom are active in the ministry. We are grateful for their love, support, and patience while we worked on this book.

Table Of Contents

Foreword

Dr. Frank and JoeNell Summerfield have the unique ability to search out and bring forth the practical meaning of spiritual truths, to carefully remove the exterior coverings of religious and spiritual clichés and clarify societies jargons that obscure spiritual, emotional and physical realities that plague the before and after of marriages. Thousands have preached and taught on marriage but few have exposed us to the spiritual depths of being happily married as the Summerfield's. They will open your eyes to the reflected Glory of God inside you as you have never seen before.

Singles Prepare Before You Say I Do is a breath of fresh air for discouraged and disheartened people, believers and non-believers a like, who feel trapped in a mundane and mediocre existence. Their insight on marriage can reside in each of us as one of the perfect prescription to inject new life and hope into weary hearts and infuse fresh excitement.

They have written what I sincerely hope will become the manifesto for a new generation of forever I do marriages. And I'm declaring them the first of what I hope will become a long line of "Marriage Planners." As the Summerfield's will remind us in the text, there are people who actually make their living as "wedding planners." But the couples who pay these people appear to expect life after their weddings to happen--magically. And we wonder why the divorce rate is so high. Well it's time that changed.

Don't just read this book, Devour it. Ingest and digest it like the bittersweet book given to John in the Revelation. You will find it informative, entertaining, humorous, and maybe a bit alarming. It will be sweet to the taste. But as you endeavor to do what you read, it may grow a bit bitter. That's good. It should trouble you. Hopefully, it will stir you to action. Hopefully, it will challenge you to prepare.

Marriage is no fairy tale. And happily ever after's don't just happen. Dr. Frank & JoeNell Summerfield have spent more than thirty years proving the principles you are about to read. Prince or princess, finding or being found, you need to plan, not just a wedding, but also a marriage. Let *Singles Prepare Before You Say I Do* be your guide. And may you, indeed, live happily ever after.

Bishop J.C. Hash, Senior Pastor
St. Peters World Outreach Center
Winston Salem, North Carolina

Our Assignment

For which of you, intending to build a tower,
sitteth not down first, and counteth the cost,
whether he have sufficient to finish it?
Lest haply, after he hath laid the foundation,
and is not able to finish it,
all that behold it begin to mock him, Saying,
This man began to build, and was not able to finish.

Luke 14:28-30

Our assignment on this project is crystal clear. We want to prepare singles for marriage. If you are single, we want to help you get ready for an honorable marriage that blesses you and glorifies God. If you are married, the proven principles in this book will help you stay in and get the most out of your marriage. Either way, this is more than a notion. This is going to take some time: time to read, time to study, time to learn, time to adjust to, time to do. But remember: preparation time is never wasted time.

There are people who actually make their living as "wedding planners." But the couples that pay these people routinely expect life after their weddings to happen--magically. And we wonder why the divorce rate is so high. Hey! If you fail to plan, you plan to fail. And we don't plan to fail.

Call us "Marriage Planners." And consider this book our business card. Consider the purchase price a retainer. An investment. Consider it a down payment on a fruitful future. Think of the time you spend reading this book as seed sown that will yield the harvest of a glorious marriage. A glorious marriage is a valuable commodity in any day and age--especially this one. U. S. statistics clearly show that marriages are failing. And being a Christian doesn't seem to affect the statistics much. The divorce rate is just as high among Christians as it is in the secular world.

Hebrews 13:4 says *"marriage is honorable in all things and the bed undefiled."* If marriage is honorable, then divorce dishonors God. We'll talk more about that later, but for right now, we want to talk about preparing marriage.

Take a moment and count the cost. Are you willing to make the adjustments, the sacrifices that marriage demands? The two shall become "one flesh," the scriptures teach. But are you ready to submit yourself to the will of God and let him shape your marriage into one that pleases him?

A good marriage requires more than coming to church. And finding a spouse in church doesn't mean that you are going to find church in them. Coming to church is a good start, but is church working? Are you and your spouse-to-be applying the principles that you learn in church to your lives?

These are the kinds of questions we will ask as we endeavor to prepare singles for marriage. You need to be prepared. You need to be prepared spiritually, financially, emotionally, and domestically.

We have been married over thirty years. Much of that time has been spent in full-time ministry. Raising four children, pastoring a church, establishing a school, preaching, teaching, traveling, training, and a list of related responsibilities that boggle the mind, would challenge any marriage. There are nights when we get home late but dinner still gets on the table, our intimacy still shows up in the bedroom, bills get paid, our house is in order, and peace prevails.

We don't have any secret formulas. And we certainly don't have an army of servants. What we have is a good marriage. We understand and accept our roles both implied and expressed. And we have made the commitment to make the effort to make our marriage one that we both enjoy. By the grace of God, our marriage is good. Yours can be too.

Diligence is key. People train for everything. Sports. The arts. Careers. The list is endless. Why not for marriage? Children start preparing for Olympic gymnastics almost as soon as they can walk. This is a regimen that might last until they are in their early twenties. But a marriage is designed to last a lifetime. When do we begin to prepare for it?

Preparing singles for marriage is a huge responsibility. First of all, marriage is the only acceptable relationship through which to bring children into the world. Marriage is definitely the best vehicle through which to train up a child. Marriage is a relationship that God guarantees to grant with favor. Marriage was God's response to the first thing in creation that he called, *"not good."* *"And the Lord God said, it is not good that the man should be alone; I will make him an help meet for him"* (Genesis 2:18).

So let's get down to it. Let's get busy preparing you for marriage. Your lifestyle is going to change once you're married. Now is the time to prepare to be flexible. Someone else is going to have to fit into your life. Now is the time to prepare to adjust. Someone else is going to count you as part of his or her life. Now is the time to position yourself as an asset to your future spouse rather than a liability.

Now is the time to prepare spiritually, financially, emotionally, physically, and domestically. Now, while you are married to Jesus, take this time to prepare for marriage.

Chapter 1
The Challenge

*It is reported commonly that there is fornication among
you, and such fornication as is not so much as named
among the Gentiles, that one should have his father's wife.*

1 Corinthians 5:1

We began our book, Why Relationships & Families Fail,
by telling you, "Marriages are being destroyed. Families
are tearing up. Couples are not staying together like they
should. People are being attacked by the forces of darkness,
and their families are being destroyed by the devil." Unfor-
tunately, in the time that it has taken us to write this book,
things don't seem to have gotten any better.

Let's face it; the world has made its way into the church.
Every media driven, perverse notion about the relationship
between a man and a woman that you can imagine has surfaced among the saints.

But this is not a new phenomenon. Paul's letters to the
churches at Corinth and Ephesus make it clear that the devil
has been attacking marriage, perverting human sexuality,
and infiltrating the church for centuries.

Date Rape. Domestic Violence. Divorce. These are just a few of the atrocities our children are seeing and hearing about, not just as news and entertainment, but all too often as the grim reality of their own lives. What's worse is that our government is now being pressured by a small sector of the population to redefine marriage and sanction, support, even normalize, behavior that the Bible calls abominable.

Almost half (48%) of high school teens say they have had sex--an increase of 2% between 2005 and 2007, according to data released by the Centers for Disease Control and Prevention. During the same time period, the proportion of high school teens that say they used a condom the last time they had sex decreased 2%.

The new data is from the CDC's 2007 Youth Risk Behavior Surveillance System. The survey is administered every two years to about 14,000 high school students nationwide and contains information on high school students' sexual behavior, drug and alcohol use, and other measures.

Fully 7% of high school students report that they had sex before age 13, 15% say they have had four or more sexual partners, and 35% say they have had sex in the past three months. These three measures of sexual behavior all increased between 2005 and 2007.

At present, 8% of high school teens say they have been forced to have sex and 10% report having experienced dating violence. Both measures are essentially unchanged between 2005 and 2007.

"Raise the red alert flag," said Sarah Brown, CEO of The National Campaign to Prevent Teen and Unplanned Pregnancy. "If teens are having more sex and using contraception less often, their rates of pregnancy and birth will obviously go up. And in fact, in December 2007, the federal government announced that the teen birth rate had increased for the first time in 15 years. {Source: National Campaign to Prevent Teen Pregnancy}

What does all this mean? Perhaps it means that the age of June weddings, Hawaiian honeymoons, and three bedroom ranches with picket fences paid for by thirty year nine-to-fives that end in retirement to Florida on fully funded 401K's may just be a thing of the past. We're looking at teenaged single moms hoping against hope to one day marry an under-educated, unemployed, class H felon who doesn't have too many kids, baby mamas, or ex-wives.

It's a brave new world and if we don't start cultivating some new ground, planting some better seed, pulling some old weeds, and fending off some little foxes, tomorrow's harvest is not going to be any better.

What we don't seem to grasp is that we are challenged with a changing worldview. The covenant breakers of Romans 1 are launching an unholy offensive and wise fools are standing in the valley of indecision like so many uncircumcised Philistines railing accusations against the armies of God. It's bad enough that they don't recognize that it is only in a Christ centered nation that they have the freedom to ply their satanic trade with government protection. But now they want to bully the rest of us into agreeing that their abominations are normal.

This is our challenge. This is what we face. Marriages are being destroyed. Families are tearing up. Couples are not staying together like they should. The forces of darkness are attacking people, and their families are being destroyed by the devil. You've seen some statistics. And we've laid out some scenarios. But let's take a look at Paul's description of the situation for a moment and glean some useful insight on the particulars.

1 Corinthians 5:1

It is reported commonly that there is fornication among you, and such fornication as is not so much as named among the Gentiles, that one should have his father's wife.

First of all, not only has the world surfaced in the church, but also the church at Corinth seemed hell bent on beating the world at its own game. Paul is saying even sinners haven't gotten this bad. We know the righteous is supposed to be *"more excellent than his neighbor,"* (Proverbs 12:26) but it appears, in this case, that *"the way of the wicked"* has, indeed, seduced us. Many sinners are still reeling from the thought of pedophile priests and pastors on the down low. But Paul doesn't stop there. He goes on to let us know how to avoid such behavior in the future.

1 Corinthians 6:15-20

Know ye not that your bodies are the members of Christ? shall I then take the members of Christ, and

*make them the members of an harlot? God forbid.
What? know ye not that he which is joined to an harlot is one body? for two, saith he, shall be one flesh.
But he that is joined unto the Lord is one spirit. Flee
fornication. Every sin that a man doeth is without
the body; but he that committeth fornication sinneth
against his own body. What? know ye not that your
body is the temple of the Holy Ghost which is in you,
which ye have of God, and ye are not your own? For
ye are bought with a price: therefore glorify God in
your body, and in your spirit, which are God's.*

Paul began by making it clear that the problem he found in
Corinth was a knowledge problem. He seemed apalled. In-
credulous even. *"What? Know ye not,"* he asked. We could
ask the same thing. Don't you know who and what you are?
Hosea said, *"my people are destroyed for lack of knowledge"*
(Hosea 4:6). Has anything changed? Isn't the destruction of
the family that we now face a function of people's rejection
of the knowledge of the word of God?

Paul continued by pointing to fornication as the tool the devil used to break down relationships in the church. He high-
lighted the fact that fornication is, first of all, a sin against
the self. The devil tricks people into believing that they can
gratify themselves at someone else's expense. But Paul said,
*"he that committeth fornication sinneth against his own
body."*

Not only does fornication negatively affect our self-image,
but also it taints our relationship with God. People forget that
once we come to know Jesus, our bodies become the temple

of the Holy Ghost. How can we lay down with whores and whoremongers in/with the temple of God? People, Christians, are rejecting this knowledge. They are holding this truth in unrighteousness and it is confusing their minds.

Paul also talked about the spiritual union that takes place between a man and a harlot. And what people don't seem to realize is that these unions get multiplied and magnified with each new partner and sexual encounter. This will eventually impact marriages. Paul finishes his comments to the church at Corinth by reminding them that their bodies are not their own. He will follow through on that theme when he talks to them about marriage.

Rejection of the knowledge of the word of God, relationships destroyed by fornication, low self-esteem, desecration of the temple of God, and a soulish man that is satanically entangled with multiple partners just waiting to defile the marriage bed. These are the things that Paul pointed out the church at Corinth. He expands the list in his letter to the church at Ephesus.

Ephesians 5:1-12

> *Be ye therefore followers of God, as dear children; And walk in love, as Christ also hath loved us, and hath given himself for us an offering and a sacrifice to God for a sweetsmelling savour. But fornication, and all uncleanness, or covetousness, let it not be once named among you, as becometh saints; Neither filthiness, nor foolish talking, nor jesting, which are not convenient: but rather giving of thanks. For this*

*ye know, that no whoremonger, nor unclean person,
nor covetous man, who is an idolater, hath any inheritance in the kingdom of Christ and of God. Let
no man deceive you with vain words: for because
of these things cometh the wrath of God upon the
children of disobedience. Be not ye therefore partakers with them. For ye were sometimes darkness,
but now are ye light in the Lord: walk as children of
light: (For the fruit of the Spirit is in all goodness
and righteousness and truth;) Proving what is acceptable unto the Lord. And have no fellowship with
the unfruitful works of darkness, but rather reprove
them. For it is a shame even to speak of those things
which are done of them in secret.*

Paul begins with an admonition to follow God as dear children. He urges them to let their love for one another be a
reflection of Christ's love for the church. But then he warns
them of the challenges we all face when it comes to living
holy as we prepare for marriage.

Fornication is, once again, at the top of the list. He adds to
it, uncleanness and/or covetousness. Don't satisfy yourself
at others' expense. Don't bring filth into the temple of God.
Don't look at and long for that which is not your own. Paul
said it shouldn't be named among the saints -- not once. He
even comments on their conversation. How often do we find
foolish talking and jesting in the sanctuary of the Lord? Paul
said such things are "inconvenient." That's the same thing
he said to the church at Rome about homosexuality. Paul
said that we should be giving thanks.

In much the same way he did with the Corinthians, Paul points the Ephesians back to what they should have known. *"For this ye know,"* he reminded them, *"that no whoremonger, nor unclean person, nor covetous man, who is an idolater, hath any inheritance in the kingdom of Christ and of God. Let no man deceive you with vain words: for because of these things cometh the wrath of God upon the children of disobedience."*

If you reject knowledge long enough, you will soon forget it. James warned us to be doers of the word and not hearers only. He said that people who hear and don't do would soon forget what manner of men and women they are. Paul even warned the Ephesians about men who would try to deceive them. He issued the same warning to Timothy.

2 Timothy 3:1-7

This know also, that in the last days perilous times shall come. Paul wrote. For men shall be lovers of their own selves, covetous, boasters, proud, blasphemers, disobedient to parents, unthankful, unholy, Without natural affection, trucebreakers, false accusers, incontinent, fierce, despisers of those that are good, Traitors, heady, highminded, lovers of pleasures more than lovers of God; Having a form of godliness, but denying the power thereof: from such turn away. For of this sort are they which creep into houses, and lead captive silly women laden with sins, led away with divers lusts, Ever learning, and never able to come to the knowledge of the truth.

Can anyone deny that *"perilous times"* have come? Are not men, *"lovers of their own selves, covetous, boasters, proud, blasphemers, disobedient to parents, unthankful, unholy, without natural affection, trucebreakers, false accusers, incontinent, fierce, despisers of those that are good, traitors, heady, highminded, lovers of pleasures more than lovers of God"* (2 Timothy 3:1-4)? Don't we have people in pulpits all over this country pretending to be God's representatives who have not allowed the power of God to transform their devilish desires?

This is our challenge. This is what we face. Marriages are being destroyed. Families are tearing up. Couples are not staying together like they should. The forces of darkness are attacking people, and their families are being destroyed by the devil. And the only thing that is going to prepare singles for marriage is our willingness and ability to come to the knowledge of the truth.

Pastors Frank & JoeNell Summerfield

Chapter 2

The Solution / The Word

But all things that are reproved are made manifest by the light: for whatsoever doth make manifest is light. Wherefore he saith, Awake thou that sleepest, and arise from the dead, and Christ shall give thee light. See then that ye walk circumspectly, not as fools, but as wise, redeeming the time, because the days are evil. Wherefore be ye not unwise, but understanding what the will of the Lord is.

Ephesians 5:13-17

Paul wrote this section of his letter to the church at Ephesus in two sections. And it appears that the first twenty verses are written to singles.

The first two verses encourage us all to be *"followers of God, as dear children"* and *"to walk in love."* Verses three through thirteen highlight the shameful sins of the flesh, fornication pointing specifically to singles, and warn those waiting for marriage to "have no fellowship with the unfruitful works of darkness, but rather reprove them."

To reprove is to criticize or correct. It is to disapprove of strongly and even to expose or shine light on. You may find us doing more of that than you like in this book. But it is needed because people in the church are struggling with these problems. There are those who live one way at church and another way away from the church.

It's like some of us have twins. Husbands and wives appear to be so happy at church, but they ride home in silence. The only thing that breaks the silence is arguments that take them home to sleep in separate bedrooms. What you see at church, all too often, is not real.

There are people sitting in our congregations, for example, who appear to be heterosexual, when in reality they are homosexuals. They shout "Amen" loudly when I preach against their abominable behavior. But that is only a smoke screen.

Society's problems are now the church's problems because the world has decided to come to church. It's good that they are here, because we will preach against sin. Society won't. The only thing that is going to make a difference is the word of God. So let's take off our halos and get down to the nitty gritty. Let's deal with sin in singles so that we don't have it to deal with in marriages.

Verses fourteen through seventeen of Ephesians 5 draw us back to the will of the Lord. We know that it is God's will that all men *"be saved, and...come unto the knowledge of the truth"* (1 Timothy 2:4). But let's look at the will of God specifically as it pertains to marriage.

Genesis 1:26-28

26 And God said, Let us make man in our image, after our likeness: and let them have dominion over the fish of the sea, and over the fowl of the air, and over the cattle, and over all the earth, and over every creeping thing that creepeth upon the earth.

27 So God created man in his own image, in the image of God created he him; male and female created he them.

28 And God blessed them, and God said unto them, Be fruitful, and multiply, and replenish the earth, and subdue it: and have dominion over the fish of the sea, and over the fowl of the air, and over every living thing that moveth upon the earth.

This is so clear. God ordained that marriage be between a man and a woman. There was a time when that was a given and the challenge was to preach holiness, prosperity, and things like that. Now, we have to deal with perversions that are forcing their way out of the proverbial closet and marching proudly down main street and even up into pulpits.

We used to have to worry about keeping the brothers from fornicating with the sisters. Now, more and more people seem to be swinging both ways. We used to call it "Acey-Deucy" in Newark. Now we don't know what to call it other than an abomination. We try to know our enemy but unnatural is trying to normalize. People look nice, but everything is not fine.

The devil is infiltrating the church. But don't you be deceived by external appearances. If it's in society, it's in the church. We're talking crack, child abuse, domestic violence, and even sodomy. The difference between the world and us is that it may come in, but we will continue to preach against it.

In Genesis 1:26, God declared that man, the species, would manifest in two genders--male and female. He then gave mankind express instruction to be fruitful and multiply. It's an old argument, but it is undeniable. Homosexuals cannot reproduce. God designed humanity to procreate and perversion undermines God's plan.

We know these ideas are not "politically correct" right now, but these are more than ideas--they are the truth, and that truth is not just a concept. That truth is Jesus himself. Our Lord said, *"I am the way, the truth, and the life; no man comes to the Father but by me"* (John 14:6).

Our lawmakers may not care about truth, but we as ministers of the gospel are committed to crying loud and sparing not. Our job is to teach truth, especially to our children. Our children are being entertained (pronounced, seduced) by everything from radio, to television, to the Internet, to mobile madness. And most of the advantage that these demonically controlled devices have comes from parents being too busy doing their own thing.

During the week, schools and day cares preach to our kids. On Sunday, if we are churchgoers, the children are entrusted to children's church and nurseries. And when they are at home, too many of our children are parked in front of televisions and computers being indoctrinated by the world.

Raising children is an active responsibility. If you are going to lie down and make a baby, you had better be ready to get up and train them. The truth that we are committed to is that raising children is a full time job.

When you are single, you must focus on being prepared. Preparation means being a virtuous woman. Preparation means remaining celibate. Chastity is sexual preparation. Use that time for other things. Get fit. Educate yourself. Learn more. Earn more. When you do marry and the babies start coming you'll be glad you took the time to value yourself.

Value is a huge issue when it comes to being single. Too many women are marrying men who can barely care for themselves. If they can't care for themselves, how in the world are these characters going to care for you and your children?

And it has been our experience that such men tend to have multiple women. They are seldom good at developing godly relationships. And they are definitely no good at commitment. You don't want them when you're single and you certainly don't want to leave your husband for one of them.

Don't give up. You can't afford to break up. Work it out. United, God can bless you. And don't push your spouse into an affair either.

1 Corinthians 7:1-5

1 Now concerning the things whereof ye wrote unto me: It is good for a man not to touch a woman.

2 Nevertheless, to avoid fornication, let every man have his own wife, and let every woman have her own husband.

3 Let the husband render unto the wife due benevolence: and likewise also the wife unto the husband.

4 The wife hath not power of her own body, but the husband: and likewise also the husband hath not power of his own body, but the wife.

5 Defraud ye not one the other, except it be with consent for a time, that ye may give yourselves to fasting and prayer; and come together again, that Satan tempt you not for your incontinency.

The miracle of marriage is that it is filled with favor. *"Whoso findeth a wife findeth a good thing,"* Solomon wrote, *"and obtaineth favour of the LORD"* (Proverbs 18:22). But Jesus said that *"if a house be divided against itself, that house cannot stand"* (Matthew3:25). That is why it is so important to prepare when you are single. Establishing those truths and organizing your life will prepare you for your Boaz or your Ruth.

People are watching you. They are aware of your choices and cognizant of your character. Look at Boaz's comments to Ruth in chapter 2 verses 11 & 12 of the book that bears her name.

11 And Boaz answered and said unto her, It hath fully been shewed me, all that thou hast done unto thy mother in law since the death of thine husband: and how thou hast left thy father and thy mother, and the land of thy nativity, and art come unto a people which thou knewest not heretofore.

12 The LORD recompense thy work, and a full reward be given thee of the LORD God of Israel, under whose wings thou art come to trust."

Boaz is rich. He is respectable. Boaz can and will take good care of you and your children. But Boaz is also discriminating. He is paying attention to his surroundings. Boaz is well aware of who is prepared and who is not. You may have made some bad choices in the past, but you can begin now to prepare. You can make yourself marketable. We know that word sounds a bit less than "spiritual" but it is critical that you understand that the Boaz's of this world are shopping. Each one is looking for his Ruth. And he wants Ruth to be prepared.

You also need to realize that we are living in a world that promotes a double standard about promiscuity. That double standard is just as prevalent in the church as it is in the world. Men who have had multiple sexual exploits and fathered numerous children are seen as dashing and virile. Women who have behaved similarly are seen as loose and whorish.

Remember the woman caught in adultery? *"And the scribes and Pharisees brought unto him a woman taken in adultery; and when they had set her in the midst, they say unto him, Master, this woman was taken in adultery, in the very act"* (John 8:3,4). If they caught her *"in the very act"* it begs the question; Where was the man?

The scribes and Pharisees reminded Jesus of the Law of Moses, but they themselves seemed to have forgotten it. Jesus was not moved. They wanted to stone her. He wrote on the ground. What did he write? No one knows. But it may have been the law. Or it may have been one or more of their names. At least one of them had to be there in order to catch her in the very act. And since Proverbs 30:18, 19 says, *"There be three things which are too wonderful for me, yea, four which I know not: The way of an eagle in the air; the way of a serpent upon a rock; the way of a ship in the midst of the sea; and the way of a man with a maid."* it seems likely that one of them may have even been the man.

It's an age-old double standard, but it is the prevailing standard. Jesus addressed the error by challenging the one who was *"...without sin among you, let him first cast a stone at her"* (John 8:7).

In the act or not, they were all guilty. They were guilty of breaking the law. And they were guilty of promoting a double standard. Double or not, however, it remains the standard. Men who have had multiple sexual exploits and fathered numerous children are seen as dashing and virile. Women who have behaved similarly are seen as loose and whorish.

It's one thing for us to teach these truths. It's another thing altogether for you to be doers of the word. You have to choose. *"Fear God, and keep his commandments:"* Solomon said, *"for this is the whole duty of man"* (Ecclesiastes 12:13). Solomon was a pretty smart king. He, himself, was a product of sexual indiscretion. He knew what he was talking about. Don't play around with this stuff. And report indiscretions.

If some guy comes on to you, call him on it. Tell him; "I'm a virtuous woman. You must have me mixed up with someone else!" Stop them in their tracks. Report them and call names. People need deliverance and the Bible says, *"Them that sin rebuke before all, that others also may fear"* (1 Timothy 5:20). You may find their advances flattering. And you may find flirting exciting. But flirtations produce ungodly results. And you have to ask yourself: "Do I want a fling or a husband?"

This is serious business. You need to understand the spiritual significance of sexual activity. *"What?"* Paul asked, *"know ye not that he which is joined to an harlot is one body? for two, saith he, shall be one flesh"* (1 Corinthians 6:16). He warns us in verse 18 of the same chapter to *"Flee fornication."* Paul begged the Christians at Rome to *"present* [their] *bodies a living sacrifice, holy, acceptable unto God, which* [was their] *reasonable service"* (Romans 12:1).

You may have come out of a loose sexual tradition, but you are born again now. You are being taught the word now. You know better now. No more fornication!

Who do you love more; God, or your own flesh? Most people are not aware that all sexual encounters produce one flesh.

Most people don't know that unsanctified sex defiles the flesh. But you need to know that every choice you make concerning your sexual behavior will one day impact your marriage.

It is also important to note that purity preserves oneness with God. Would you really forsake eternity for a brief thrill that can't heal, bless, forgive, or deliver you?

Remember: Fornication is a sin against your own body. Flee fornication! Run from it. Get away. Better yet, avoid the temptation to fornicate in the first place. Let's read Ephesians 5:1-21 again to see how.

1 Be ye therefore followers of God, as dear children;

2 And walk in love, as Christ also hath loved us, and hath given himself for us an offering and a sacrifice to God for a sweetsmelling savour.

3 But fornication, and all uncleanness, or covetousness, let it not be once named among you, as becometh saints;

4 Neither filthiness, nor foolish talking, nor jesting, which are not convenient: but rather giving of thanks.

5 For this ye know, that no whoremonger, nor unclean person, nor covetous man, who is an idolater, hath any inheritance in the kingdom of Christ and of God.

6 Let no man deceive you with vain words: for because of these things cometh the wrath of God upon the children of disobedience.

7 Be not ye therefore partakers with them.

8 For ye were sometimes darkness, but now are ye light in the Lord: walk as children of light:

9 (For the fruit of the Spirit is in all goodness and righteousness and truth;)

10 Proving what is acceptable unto the Lord.

11 And have no fellowship with the unfruitful works of darkness, but rather reprove them.

12 For it is a shame even to speak of those things which are done of them in secret.

13 But all things that are reproved are made manifest by the light: for whatsoever doth make manifest is light.

14 Wherefore he saith, Awake thou that sleepest, and arise from the dead, and Christ shall give thee light.

15 See then that ye walk circumspectly, not as fools, but as wise,

16 Redeeming the time, because the days are evil.

17 Wherefore be ye not unwise, but understanding what the will of the Lord is.

18 And be not drunk with wine, wherein is excess; but be filled with the Spirit;

19 Speaking to yourselves in psalms and hymns and spiritual songs, singing and making melody in your heart to the Lord;

20 Giving thanks always for all things unto God and the Father in the name of our Lord Jesus Christ;

21 Submitting yourselves one to another in the fear of God.

To you who are single, God's word is clear. Follow God. Flee fornication. Reprove evil. Wake up and seek the will of God.

God intended for men and women to marry, be fruitful, and multiply. God intended for the union between a man and woman to be blessed and covered by his favor. But there is nothing in the scriptures that requires that people marry.

Marriage is not a requirement for salvation.

Paul actually taught that is was better not to marry. *"So then he that giveth her in marriage doeth well;"* he said, *"but he that giveth her not in marriage doeth better"* (1 Corinthians 7:38). Why? Because: *"He that is unmarried careth for the things that belong to the Lord, how he may please the Lord:*

But he that is married careth for the things that are of the world, how he may please his wife" (1 Corinthians 7:32, 33).

So where does that leave us? It leaves us with two decisions. Are we prepared to face the challenges of marriage? And if so, are we prepared to face them according to the word of God? Ephesians 5:21 is a powerful transition statement for singles preparing for marriage. *"Submitting yourselves one to another in the fear of God."*

It is only the fear of God that will cause men and women to submit to one another and it is only the fear of God that will enable a man to love his wife and a woman to reverence her husband. The word of God is the only thing that can help men and women effectively face the challenges that marriages are facing today.

40

Pastors Frank & JoeNell Summerfield

Chapter 3

Singles

*Marriage is honourable in all, and the bed undefiled:
but whoremongers and adulterers God will judge.*

Hebrews 13:4

Marriage is honorable. That means marriage is fruitful, productive, accommodating, mutually gratifying, fulfilling, sustaining, preserving. If that is true, then we have to ask: Why are so many marriages terminated? The answer is simple.

It is impossible to have successful marriages without first addressing the dysfunctional behavior patterns of the single people who will one day marry.

If you are single, you are married to God. Jesus Christ is your husband and the time you have with him prior to meeting and marrying your earthly husband or wife is time that should be spent to pay attention to some critical areas in your life. Address them now, because any issues you don't address while you are single will only be aggravated by marriage.

We are talking to two kinds of people now. People who know they have issues. And people who don't know. The people who know they have issues have to make the decision to deal with their issues or remain alone. The people who don't know they have issues need to be made aware of their issues and then they have to make the decision to deal with their issues or remain alone.

When you are single, you are unconfined. You have no responsibility for anyone but yourself. You are not accountable to anyone but yourself. When you get married, someone else has a say. When you get married you have to deal with your issues. When it's just you, there's no problem. No one challenges you. But when you get married questions arise.

Suppose you don't manage money well. If you marry someone who is a stickler about money, counting every penny, you are going to have problems. They are not going to sit by quietly and watch you throw away their money or yours. They have that part of their lives together, but something else is probably wrong or they wouldn't have married you to begin with. People tend to marry at or above their own level. I know you've heard that opposites attract, but most of us look for certain areas of compatibility.

We can talk all we please, but singles with unresolved issues are still going to get married. They are going to make a public covenant. God will put them together. But many of them will go on to put the covenant asunder.

There will also be some couples that will make it. They will work on their lives as singles and apply those same principles to their marriage. Take John and Alice for example. Jay was a changed man when he realized that he had found a wife. He should have been. Solomon said, a man that *"findeth a wife findeth a good thing, and obtaineth favour of the LORD"* (Proverbs 18:22). That favor is important, because it applies God's grace to all that you do. And no man needs a wife unless he is doing something. By the time Adam found Eve he already had an assignment.

Too many couples get it backwards. Men want to find a wife before they have found their calling. We're not just talking about ministry calling. What is it that God wants you to do with your life? If you don't know what to do with your life, you won't know what to do with your wife.

John and Alice had plenty of interaction at church before they decided to get married. They were friends first. Then there was a period of courtship. Before the decision was made to marry, they sought wise counsel. Finally they married.

The most important thing they did before marrying, however was to prepare as singles. Let's look at some areas where all singles need to prepare before considering marriage.

Spiritually

The Bible is very clear about not being *"unequally yoked"* (2 Corinthians 6:14). You should not even consider marrying someone who is not born again. For those of you who are mature in the Lord, you want your spouse to be Spirit-filled and Spirit-led. You should never marry someone who is not as excited about going to church as you are. And it is best that husbands and wives go to the same church. Finally, you both need to be in the word and doers of the word. It is the word of God that will best prepare you for marriage.

Financially

Marriages need finances to survive. We need to say that again. Marriages need finances to survive. You can not live on love alone. One of the greatest causes of divorce in America is disputes over money, usually the lack of it. Men, you need a job, a sustainable source of income, before you get married. Men and women need to do their very best to get out of debt before they get married. Debt creates a burden that is difficult to bear for any marriage. If you have debts, you should make your future spouse aware of them going into the marriage.

You are going to need somewhere to live. The married man is instructed to *"leave his father and his mother, and shall cleave unto his wife"* (Genesis 2:24). If you're going to get married, you're going to need a house. Jesus said, *"I go to prepare a place for you"* (John14:2). No respectable Jewish man can get married until his father approves of the accommodations he has prepared for his bride.

You are going to need viable transportation. How will you get to work? How will you get to church? How will your kids get to school? These are all things you must consider before you get married.

Emotionally

Too many people see marriage as an opiate to dull the pain of their personal self-esteem problems. Love does not satisfy itself at the expense of others. Love gives. *"For God so loved the world, he gave..."* (John 3:16). It is unfair to expect someone else to shoulder the burden of your low self-esteem. No man or woman can make you "feel good" about yourself forever.

The intimacy of marriage will expose all your inhibitions. If you are not ready to have those flaws revealed, you are not ready to be married. We will talk more about this when we get to domestic issues, but you have to ask yourself: "How can I hang on to my hang-ups if my body is not my own?"

If you have been married before or in multiple relationships, you must be sure you have dealt with all your unresolved issues. It is not fair to hold your current spouse hostage to the faults of your ex. Deal with your issues before you get married.

Domestically

Love is grand, but marriage can get real practical. Are you ready to keep a clean house? Are you prepared for consistent sexual intimacy? Can you handle the challenge of paying bills, even ones you didn't make? Can you manage a household, and a life that is filled with other people? And what will you do when it's time to raise children?

All of these issues will be affected by your understanding of the individual roles & expectations each of you bring to the marriage. Should the man be the sole breadwinner? Should the wife be the primary care giver? Who has the last word in major decisions? These are all questions that both of you must have compatible answers to.

At the end of the day, all marriages require adaptability. You have to be willing to adjust. You have to be willing to change.

Chapter 4

Hard To Find

Whoso findeth a wife findeth a good thing,
and obtaineth favour of the LORD.

Proverbs 18:22

At about the same time our children go off to college, they are also beginning to think about issues of sex, dating, and marriage. The problem is, our college campuses tend to be havens for things that make Spirit-led decisions difficult. Alcohol. Substance Abuse. Promiscuity. Perversion. Secular Humanism.

Our kids are faced with the challenge of enjoying the liberty of their newfound freedom without being trapped in the bondage of a new worldview.

Imagine being seventeen or eighteen and having to think about things like date rape, abortion, STD's & HIV. These are children who have a lot of book sense, but often very little common or Spiritual sense. They've got great GPA's, but their awareness of how the world works is MIA. And it's not just the kids. There are professors teaching while they are stoned. There are people in authority preying on youthful inexperience in order to satisfy their own lusts.

We are living in a world where promiscuity is purposeful. High School girls are forming pregnancy clubs. Public high schools have nursery & daycare programs, paid for by our property taxes to accommodate the high percentage of teen-aged mothers in certain communities. And what is all this promiscuity about? Rejecting God.

Romans 1:18

18 For the wrath of God is revealed from heaven against all ungodliness and unrighteousness of men, who hold the truth in unrighteousness;

19 Because that which may be known of God is manifest in them; for God hath shewed it unto them.

20 For the invisible things of him from the creation of the world are clearly seen, being understood by the things that are made, even his eternal power and Godhead; so that they are without excuse:

21 Because that, when they knew God, they glorified him not as God, neither were thankful; but became vain in their imaginations, and their foolish heart was darkened.

22 Professing themselves to be wise, they became fools,

23 And changed the glory of the uncorruptible God into an image made like to corruptible man, and to birds, and fourfooted beasts, and creeping things.

47

24 Wherefore God also gave them up to uncleanness through the lusts of their own hearts, to dishonour their own bodies between themselves:

25 Who changed the truth of God into a lie, and worshipped and served the creature more than the Creator, who is blessed for ever. Amen.

26 For this cause God gave them up unto vile affections: for even their women did change the natural use into that which is against nature:

27 And likewise also the men, leaving the natural use of the woman, burned in their lust one toward another; men with men working that which is unseemly, and receiving in themselves that recompence of their error which was meet.

28 And even as they did not like to retain God in their knowledge, God gave them over to a reprobate mind, to do those things which are not convenient;

29 Being filled with all unrighteousness, fornication, wickedness, covetousness, maliciousness; full of envy, murder, debate, deceit, malignity; whisperers,

30 Backbiters, haters of God, despiteful, proud, boasters, inventors of evil things, disobedient to parents,

31 Without understanding, covenantbreakers, without natural affection, implacable, unmerciful:

32 Who knowing the judgment of God, that they which commit such things are worthy of death, not only do the same, but have pleasure in them that do them.

As if that weren't enough, our government is trying desperately to make it illegal for us to preach against such behavior.

The Local Law Enforcement Hate Crimes Prevention Act, S.909, for example, is currently being considered by the Senate. It has already passed the House as H.R. 1913. It will expand current federal hate crime laws to include sexual orientation and gender identity. It has also been dubbed the Pedophile Protection Act because an amendment to exclude pedophiles as a protected class was struck down.

If passed, the law will put clergy at risk of prosecution if they preach a Biblical message against the sin of homosexuality and someone who hears it goes out and commits a crime against a homosexual. What are our young people to do? How will they ever prepare for marriage in such an environment?

We asked some of the young men and women in our church what they were looking for in a husband or a wife. When you consider the media's persistent pressure to convince us that everybody's a pimp or a whore or a homosexual or a lesbian, you might find their answers surprising.

Our sons want wives who can cook and clean and manage a household. They want regular intimacy with their wives and good relationships with their children. And they don't want their wives to have been with anyone else before them.

Our daughters want responsible men who will work hard, pay bills and establish a decent home for them. They want a protector who will keep them and their children safe.

Looks are important to our children, but not as important as you might think. Our children care about character and integrity. Most of all, they want their lifetime companions to be saved. Even sinners know to look for husbands and wives at church. Just watch "Coming To America" or listen to Rick James. You don't take the "Super Freaks" home to mother. A bar is no place to find a wife. Party girls are good for a weekend fling, but purity is the stuff of longevity.

Why, because marriage should elevate. Marriage should take you to the next level. You should grow when you marry. You should improve when you say "I do." Your life should get better exponentially when you add another life to it. Remember Proverbs 18:22. *"Whoso findeth a wife findeth a good thing, and obtaineth favour of the LORD."*

The problem is, good husbands and wives are not so easily found. Solomon asked the question: *"Who can find a virtuous woman"* (Proverbs 31:10)? That was almost three thousand years ago. It seems that the search is becoming more difficult as time goes by. But we can change that.

Be good. Get better. Improve in every area of your life. Control your conversation. Monitor your dress. What you wear and how you wear it are outward expressions of your intelligence and your integrity. Continually flaunting your body in form fitting clothing sends a message to all who see you. And it may not be the message you intend.

Your behavior is important as well. Use your single time to develop prior to marriage. Improve. Enhance. Grow. Leave your comfort zone. Challenge yourself. And become the kind of person you would like to find for yourself.

Attraction is not merely a physical thing. When we met, we were attracted physically, but there was an intellectual attraction also. There was this ongoing curiosity. We both wanted to know what the other knew. That was exciting. It still is. Bodies change. You may try to fight it, but age--and gravity--have a powerful pull on physical appearance.

India Airie wrote a song called, *Can you be a part of my life*. In it, she talks about the temporary pleasures of casual relationships, but as she matured she began to think about longevity. You need to do the same thing. Why would you want to be with someone who only wants to take off your clothes? That is so shallow. That is sick. That is sad. Surely you realize that you are more valuable than that.

Marriage should not create struggle. So live your life in a way that attracts quality. Carry yourself in a way that invites peace. Take another look at Ruth and her first encounter with Boaz and you'll see what we mean.

Ruth 2:10-12

10 Then she fell on her face, and bowed herself to the ground, and said unto him, Why have I found grace in thine eyes, that thou shouldest take knowledge of me, seeing I am a stranger?

11 And Boaz answered and said unto her, It hath fully been shewed me, all that thou hast done unto thy mother in law since the death of thine husband: and how thou hast left thy father and thy mother, and the land of thy nativity, and art come unto a people which thou knewest not heretofore.

12 The LORD recompense thy work, and a full reward be given thee of the LORD God of Israel, under whose wings thou art come to trust.

Boaz knew of Ruth's character. He knew of her loyalty. And he knew of her work ethic. Was she beautiful? Perhaps. The scriptures don't describe her. But Boaz was a businessman and he knew that beauty depreciates. He was looking for qualities that would get better with time. He wanted a wife that would make him better. The same qualities were important to Isaac, the son of Abraham.

Abraham sent his chief steward to find a wife for his son. After praying that God would show him the right woman, this servant picked Rebekah. Listen to his prayer prior to meeting her.

Genesis 24:13,14

13 Behold, I stand here by the well of water; and the daughters of the men of the city come out to draw water:

14 And let it come to pass, that the damsel to whom I shall say, Let down thy pitcher, I pray thee, that I may drink; and she shall say, Drink, and I will give thy camels drink also: let the same be she that thou hast appointed for thy servant Isaac; and thereby shall I know that thou hast shewed kindness unto my master.

Was Rebekah beautiful? Undoubtedly. Genesis 26:7 says that "she was fair to look upon." But physical beauty was not the litmus test for marital suitability. Abraham's servant knew that his master valued character, integrity, generosity, hard work, and holiness. Rebekah had such a servant's heart that her hospitality caused the steward to worship God. (See Genesis 24:26)

Isn't that what marriage is supposed to do? Aren't we admonished to submit ourselves one to another in the fear of God? Shouldn't our husbands and wives be the kind of people that provoke us to worship God? We need to teach these things to our children early because it really is hard to teach old dogs new tricks.

We need to teach our sons how to find a virtuous woman. And we need to prepare our daughters to get found.

One last word on this subject--especially to our daughters. Don't appear needy. Rely on God. Worship God. Trust God. Spend your single time being consistently intimate with God. Remember the sacredness of marriage. Maximize it. Cherish it. Relish it. Don't abuse it.

Finally to our sons and daughters; once you have found or been found, value the gift. Be careful in your speech to one another. Ephesians 4:29 says, *"Let no corrupt communication proceed out of your mouth, but that which is good to the use of edifying, that it may minister grace unto the hearers."* Guys, you have found a *"good thing."* Edify your good thing. Build her up. Enhance her with your words. Advance her with your actions. Encourage one another and that which is good will get better and better.

Girls, watch your mouths. Boisterous and loud were good for the club. You needed that to rise above the noise. But vile and vulgar are not what husbands are looking for. Peter understood what is attractive in a woman's conversation; *"...even the ornament of a meek and quiet spirit, which is in the sight of God of great price"* (1 Peter 3:4). God don't like ugly, and neither do husbands.

A meek and quiet spirit is the product of the Holy Spirit. Let him lead you to your wife. Let him reveal you to your husband. And ask questions. Don't get distracted by surface physical beauty. You are going to be with this person 'til one of you dies. Poke around. Kick the tires. Provoke some answers. It is worth the effort, because good husbands and wives are hard to find.

Chapter 5

Unequally Yoked

Be ye not unequally yoked together with unbelievers: for what fellowship hath righteousness with unrighteousness? and what communion hath light with darkness?

2 Corinthians 6:14

People in our churches are born again but still bound. Like Lazarus coming forth from the tomb, they need their grave clothes removed. That simple truth is impacting couples before and after they get married. And much of the impact is manifest in the spouses they choose.

If you don't apply some discipline to your Christian experience, you will be easily deceived. And the worst form of deception is self-deception. If you don't know and do the word of God, you are at serious risk of marrying the wrong person.

James 1:22-24

22 But be ye doers of the word, and not hearers only, deceiving your own selves.

23 For if any be a hearer of the word, and not a doer, he is like unto a man beholding his natural face in a glass:

24 For he beholdeth himself, and goeth his way, and straightway forgetteth what manner of man he was.

Matters of the heart tend to make us forgetful. We forget who we are. We forget whose we are. Sometimes we even forget that God has not forgotten us. This is an ongoing problem, and marriage only compounds single problems.

Remember: Forgetfulness leads to self-deception and the only protection we have against forgetfulness is commitment. We have to remain committed to doing the word of God. If you don't want to be deceived, especially self-deceived, you had better commit to doing the word of God--NOW.

We began this book by reminding you that if you fail to plan, you plan to fail. So what is your plan? Do you have some structure in place for your marriage? Do you have your career on track? These are the kind of plans you need to be thinking about while you are single. These are the kind of commitments that will help to fend off deception. And just so there is no mistaking what we are talking about: If forgetfulness while you're single leads to deception, then it is fair to say that marriages born of that deception often end in divorce.

We told you we don't plan to fail. You shouldn't plan to fail either. Begin by making a commitment to God's definition of marriage. That means no divorce. When the honeymoon is over and the romance leaves the marriage, you will go home because you are committed. When two committed people become one, they are both committed to the standard that the only acceptable exit from a marriage is death. Settle that when you're single and marry someone who has made the same commitment and you drastically lower the chance of divorce. Also make a committment and decree that you will both stay married and live till Jesus comes. Stand on Mark 11:22-24 and Proverbs 18:20-21.

The next thing you need to do is agree on the rules. Marriage is, in many ways, like a game. You would be surprised at how many people either don't know or refuse to play by the rules. Maybe that's why they call being unfaithful to a spouse -- cheating.

The rules for marriage are found in the Bible. God invented marriage and he determined the object of the game and he made the rules.

The object is found in Genesis 1:28

> *Be fruitful, and multiply, and replenish the earth, and subdue it: and have dominion over the fish of the sea, and over the fowl of the air, and over every living thing that moveth upon the earth.*

The rules start in Genesis and can be found throughout the Bible.

Genesis 1:27,28 lets us know that a marriage consists of one man and one woman. *"...male and female created he them."*

Men and women have tried to change this rule over the years and God has winked at their disobedience from time to time. But Jesus reminded the Pharisees and us *"from the beginning of the creation God made them male and female. For this cause,"* Jesus said *"shall a man leave his father and mother, and cleave to his wife; And they twain shall be one flesh: so then they are no more twain, but one flesh. What therefore God hath joined together, let not man put asunder."* Divorce is against the rules. But let's not get ahead of ourselves. Since we are really talking to singles preparing for marriage, let's look at the rules as they pertain to what should happen before marriage. We'll call this the pre-game warm up. (Or maybe cool down is a better description.)

1 Corinthians 7:1,2

1 Now concerning the things whereof ye wrote unto me: It is good for a man not to touch a woman.

2 Nevertheless, to avoid fornication, let every man have his own wife, and let every woman have her own husband.

So many singles want to rush toward sexual intimacy before they get married. Most of them don't intend to wind up in fornication any more than a golfer intends to wind up in a hazard. But if you don't know the rules, you will seldom be good at any game.

Paul wrote this letter to the church at Corinth while he was in prison. He was in prison and they were in trouble. Perhaps you remember his comments about the man who had fornicated with his father's wife. He accused the Corinthians of being "puffed up," when, in his opinion, they should have "mourned" this behavior.

This man was breaking the rules. The church was ignoring the rules. And Paul was reminding them of the rules. In verses 9-13 of 1 Corinthians 5 Paul reminds the church that he has written to them before. He begins to make the distinction between worldly sinners and people who claim to be Christians but are living in sin. His instruction is *"not to company with fornicators."*

Paul is writing to Christians. Paul is writing to the church. We are writing to the same crowd because the same situation exists in the church today. People are unequally yoked.

Jesus said, *"Take my yoke upon you, and learn of me; for I am meek and lowly in heart: and ye shall find rest unto your souls. For my yoke is easy, and my burden is light"* (Matthew 11:29,30).

Remember we said that marriage is honorable and honorable means productive, accommodating, mutually gratifying, fulfilling, sustaining, preserving? When your marriage is all of these things, the burden is light because the yoke is easy. You are yoked to Jesus and your spouse is yoked to Jesus and everyone is walking together in agreement.

When you are married to an unbeliever, you are unequally yoked. You are yoked to Jesus. Your spouse is yoked to his father the devil. (See John 8:48) Jesus and the Holy Spirit are trying to lead you on a spiritual path while the devil is pulling your spouse, to whom you are bound, by his flesh in the opposite direction.

Paul said, *"the flesh lusteth against the Spirit, and the Spirit against the flesh: and these are contrary the one to the other: so that ye cannot do the things that ye would"* (Galatians 5:17). When you are married to an unbeliever, it is difficult to serve the Lord. You want to serve God and your spouse wants to serve the devil. And there was evidence of this before you got married.

Maybe you were unsaved when you got married and have given your life to the Lord since then. Your spouse has yet to catch up and you feel stuck because the new rules say no divorce. The saddest cases we see are cases where a saint knowingly marries a sinner. Maybe the sinner put on a good act before the wedding. Maybe she came to church with you and seemed interested in the things of God. But the signs were probably all around you as well. You just ignored the rules.

There's an old story about a woman who was walking home from church on an icy winter afternoon. She heard a noise from the bushes crying,

"Help me! Help me!"

When she looked down, there was a snake freezing to death. At first she was frightened, but the milk of human kindness rose up in her and compassion stopped her in her tracks.

The snake, knowing that she was vulnerable, said,

"I'm dying. Please pick me up and put me in your bosom so that I can thaw out."

The woman's fears quickly rose and she replied.

"I will not. You will bite me."

The snake assured her that he would never do such a thing.

"Please. Please. I won't bite you. If you save my life I will be forever greatful. Please don't let me die."
The woman thought for a moment and pressed for further assurance.

"Are you sure you won't bite me?"

The snake promised.

"On my life, I will be your friend forever. I'll even protect you from other snakes. Please, don't let me die."

Move by his feigned sincerity and seduced by the thought of not having to fear snakes ever again, the woman picked up the trembling snake and placed him gently in her bosom. As she walked the snake began to revive from her warmth. Just as she began to grow comfortable with his presence on her flesh, the venomous beast bit her right on her breast.

"Aaaaaaagh! She screamed. You bit me. You bit."

As the serpent slithered down her leg, leaving her far from help, to die, he replied.

"You knew I was a snake when you picked me up."

The rules are in place to protect us. The scriptures help us to identify a snake when we see one. The word of God highlights lies and stabilizes us with truth. So, when a serpent slithers into our lives and asks, "Hath God said?" we can reply with authority and not be moved by our emotions.

Here are a few rules that will keep you from marrying an unbeliever.

Stay away from fornicators.

1 Corinthians 5:9-11

9 I wrote unto you in an epistle not to company with fornicators:

10 Yet not altogether with the fornicators of this world, or with the covetous, or extortioners, or with idolaters; for then must ye needs go out of the world.

11 But now I have written unto you not to keep company, if any man that is called a brother be a fornicator, or covetous, or an idolator, or a railer, or a drunkard, or an extortioner; with such an one no not to eat.

Notice: This warning is to Christians about other Christians. These are people in the church who are still engaging in activities that are ungodly. The minute a man makes a sexual advance toward you cut him loose. If he expresses his desire to satisfy himself at your expense, he is a covetous man and cannot be trusted. If he tries to manipulate you, threatening to leave, or questioning your maturity, he is an extortioner. If he claims to love you more than anything else, he is a liar and an idolator.

People like this will have other habits too. Our mothers and grandmothers used to tell us; if he'll lie, he'll steal. And if he'll steal, he'll kill. If you let the devil ride in your car, pretty soon he's going to want to drive. Watch for temper tantrums and various forms of intoxication. If a man is pressuring you to violate the word of God, get away from him. Paul says you ought not even eat with him.

No touching

1 Corinthians 7:1,2

1 Now concerning the things whereof ye wrote unto me: It is good for a man not to touch a woman.

2 Nevertheless, to avoid fornication, let every man have his own wife, and let every woman have her own husband.

The devil is cunning. The Bible says his greatest weapon is seduction. He won't just jump out of the bushes in a red suit with a pitchfork and hit you in the head. He comes as *"an angel of light"* (2 Corinthians 11:14).

Women will bat their eyes at you and tell you how handsome you are. They will snuggle up against you and expect you to comfort them when they need it. "Hold me. I'm cold or frightened." They'll say. Don't do it. Every touch, every kiss, every caress is leading you further away from your convictions and your God. Our dear friend, Apostle Donald Q. Fozard calls it, "upper persuasion for a lower invasion" in his book Sexual Sins -- The devil's hit men.

We know it's the twenty-first century. And we know it sounds extreme. But the rules are clear. "It is good for a man not to touch a woman."

Avoid the appearance of evil

1 Thessalonians 5:22

Abstain from all appearance of evil.

Single women, you have to be mindful of appearances. What are your neighbors to think when men are coming in and out of your house or apartment at all hours of the night and day? Pastors and leaders, how can you avoid scandal if you are constantly "counseling" unaccompanied women behind closed doors?

There was a song in the seventies that expressed a lot of wisdom in this regard.

"It's not what you look like, when you're doin what you're doin. It's what you're doin when you're doin what you look like you're doin!

Well, we'd liked to express a more Biblical idea.

If it looks like you're doing what people think you are doing it won't be long 'til you're doing what they thought you were doing. Suppress yourself.

Solomon asked a serious question. *"Can a man take fire in his bosom, and his clothes not be burned"* (Proverbs 6:27)? The answer is, NO! Don't even give the appearance of evil.

Watch what you say

1 Corinthians 15:33

Be not deceived: evil communications corrupt good manners.

Everything begins with words. Read Genesis 1, John 1, and Hebrews ll. Words are how God created the world. And your words are framing your world as well. Those sweet nothings are not nothing. Jesus said, *"out of the abundance of the heart the mouth speaketh"* (Matthew 12:34).

That violent man warned you before he hit you. You just didn't believe him. You thought he was just playing, but his temper was revealed in his words. That cheater expressed his desire to be with your friend before she cheated. You just didn't believe her. You thought she was just a flirt. Pay attention to people's words. Words frame worlds.

If the people you are hanging around love to talk trash, sooner or later you are going to have to clean it up.

One time is too many...

Ephesians 5:3

But fornication, and all uncleanness, or covetousness, let it not be once named among you, as becometh saints;

Patterns and habits are developed one action at a time. If you allow them to persist, you will look back and they will constitute your life. It's not "just once." Every one of those "onces" is painting a picture.

Our churches are filled with people who have been in multiple relationships or marriages. The traditional family has been attacked so much that we are inventing names to describe the messes we have made. Step children. Blended families. These were never God's plan.

If you're already there, there is no condemnation now that you're in Christ Jesus. But for those of you that are single and unscathed, remember: you are just one decision from being unequally yoked.

Chapter 6

Ask Questions

From whence come wars and fightings among you?
come they not hence, even of your lusts that war in your
members? Ye lust, and have not: ye kill,
and desire to have, and cannot obtain:
ye fight and war, yet ye have not, because ye ask not.

James 4:1,2

A lot of trouble could be avoided in marriages if single people would spend less time kissing and more time asking questions. The time between attraction and commitment should be one big interview. This is the person you are considering spending the rest of your life with. This is the person that is going to sire and train your children. This is the person that is going to inherit all your money if you die. Ask questions. Ask hard questions. Ask questions that address what is important to you.

Even God encourages us to ask questions. Jesus said, *"Ask, and it shall be given you; seek, and ye shall find; knock, and it shall be opened unto you. For every one that asketh receiveth; and he that seeketh findeth; and to him that knocketh it shall be opened"* (Luke 11:9,10).

Let's go back to chapter 3 and use the areas we said you needed to be prepared in as a guide for developing a questionnaire for potential spouses.

We're not going to just ask questions. We are going to know what the Bibles says the answers to the questions ought to be. And then, we are going to compare the answers to actions. Are you doing what you say, or are you just trying to deceive me with your words? The queen of Sheba proved Solomon with *"hard questions"* (1 Kings 10:1) and she was just visiting. You are talking about living with someone for the rest of your life.

Habakkuk 2:2

And the LORD answered me, and said, Write the vision, and make it plain upon tables, that he may run that readeth it.

Vision (Plan)

When God decided to make man, he had a plan in mind. He didn't just form Adam and place him in the garden. He had an expectation concerning his creation. He has an expectation concerning you, too. He says, *"I know the thoughts that I think toward you, saith the LORD, thoughts of peace, and not of evil, to give you an expected end"* (Jeremiah 29:11).

What kind of end do you expect? What is your future husband thinking? You won't know until you ask.

Spirituality

Are you Born Again? You have to begin with this question. This is a deal breaker. Has this person repented of their sins, asked God's forgiveness, and been willing to change? Take them to the scriptures. Don't accept answers like, "I'm a good person." Or, "I'm doing better now." You don't want to marry anyone that isn't saved.

Are you Spirit-Filled? Chances are if you're reading this book, you have some connection to our ministry. Ours is a Spirit-filled ministry. We have our roots in Pentecost and we speak with other tongues. If you are a tongue talker and you believe in the gifts and fruit of the Spirit, you probably want to be married to someone who flows that way too. You don't want your wife looking at you funny every time you praise God. Point that woman to 2 Samuel 6 and remind her of God's judgment on Michal.

What church will we belong to after we're married? You may not meet your future spouse at your local church. If you don't, one of you is going to have a decision to make. First of all, make sure they are actively involved in their church. You don't just want a churchgoer, because you are not just a churchgoer. You don't want to have to drag your husband to church. And you don't want your wife badgering you because you stay at church too long. Church membership is an important part of marriage.

Are you at tither? This may be one of the most important questions you ask. Your financial future is tied to the answer to this question. And one of the primary causes for divorce in America is problems with money--usually lack of it. The Bible says that a man that will not bring all the tithe and the offering into the storehouse is a thief and a robber. (See Malachi 3:8-12) Paul said no thief shall inherit the kingdom of God. (See 1 Corinthians 6:10)

Unwillingness to tithe will bring a curse upon your house. So don't play around with this. Ask to see the checkbook. Watch him at offering time. Is he cheerful? Does she look for ways to give? Or is she stingy? Does she make excuses and complain about giving? Don't mince words here. All of this will impact your future. The devourer (Satan) gains access to our homes through our failure to tithe.

Financial Stability

People in love tend to make light of financial matters. They spout clichés and ignore truth. "The best things in life are free." "Money can't buy happiness." "Love is all you need." Well, the man that sang, "Love is all you need" was quite rich when he said it. You're going to need money and lots of it when you're married. Raising children is expensive. Food. Gas. Rent. A Mortgage. Insurance. Health Care. None of these things can be paid for with love. You are going to need some money.

Where do you work? The Bible says, *"if any would not work, neither should he eat"* (2 Thessalonians 3:10). You can't afford to take promises on this. Women tend to marry men based on their potential. Potential is fine, but there ought to be some evidence of a beginning before you commit yourself to a promised end. Ask. Where do your work?

How much do you make? We tend to be a little squeamish about these kinds of questions. People know that, so they lie to us. Men put on a good show when they are pursuing women, but many of them wind up being all hat and no cattle. Ask. How much do you make? What is your salary? Did your business turn a profit last year? How much of your earnings do you bring home?

How much debt do you have? Working is fine and paychecks are good, but debt can neutralize every effort and leave a family frustrated. It is not fair to burden someone else with the bondage of debt without his or her knowledge. We demand full disclosure from elected officials, why not our spouses? Debt doesn't have to be a deal breaker, but you have to have a plan.

Where are we going to live when we're married? We reminded you earlier that Jesus went to prepare a place for us. He was just imitating his Father who prepared a place for the first Adam. If a man has to take you to his mother's on your honeymoon, he is not ready to marry you.

How will we get from place to place? We no longer live in a walking world. If you live in a pedestrian friendly city, like New York, NY, you might be able to make it without a car. But in most US cities a married couple needs two reliable vehicles. Going everywhere together may seem romantic while you're dating, but relying on someone else or being relied on by someone else for transportation with run out of gas fast once you're married.

Do you have any insurance? Young people think they are invincible. They don't think about getting sick or hurt, and they believe they are going to live forever. We believe in healing, but certain preparations are completely Biblical. The "Good Samaritan" of Luke 10 paid a hospital bill to help a stranger who had been mugged. Too many Americans have to rely on the charity of others when the devil attacks them.

How many women have lost their homes and savings behind an uninsured husband who died unexpectedly? Abraham buried Sarah in style. Who is going to bury you? Ask to see the policy and make sure the premiums get paid.

Ruth 1:16,17

16 And Ruth said, Intreat me not to leave thee, or to return from following after thee: for whither thou goest, I will go; and where thou lodgest, I will lodge: thy people shall be my people, and thy God my God:

17 Where thou diest, will I die, and there will I be buried: the LORD do so to me, and more also, if ought but death part thee and me.

When you marry someone, you marry their past, their present, and their future. You marry their family, their friends, and everyone they are connected too. You marry every scar. You marry every choice. Every hidden fear your intended has becomes a part of your experience. Ruth understood that and committed herself to Naomi's choices, home, God, and coffin.

Emotional Stability

Questions may not be as effective here as keen observation. But the most important question may be; *When can I meet your parents?* Or let's spend some time with your friends? Ask to visit grandma and crazy old uncle George.

Watch for schism and strife between siblings. Look for acts of kindness toward nieces and nephews. And be sure to pay attention to how your intended responds to pressure. Emotional stability has a huge bearing on relationships and you can only predict how your future spouse will treat you by watching how he treats others.

Domesticity

Should you decide to marry, you have to plan for life after the honeymoon. People spend a lot of time planning weddings, but they seldom think about the practical issues of life's daily grind. The question here might be; *What does your week look like?*

Do you cook? Are you a clean freak or a slob? Do you pay your bills on time? Are you a good manager of money? Do you want children? How many? Do you believe in spanking or are you a Time Out person?

Answers to these questions will reveal patterns. But there is another question that will shed light on expectations. A man may eat most of his meals in restaurants because he can't cook or his job makes certain domestic duties difficult to manage. But that man may be expecting his wife to pick up the slack. What will you do with that expectation if you have a demanding career as well?

You won't get answers to all of your questions in one sitting. Some answers will be revealed over time. But you have to ask the questions. It may be uncomfortable. It may be embarrassing. But we are talking about your life. Take time to prepare before you marry. Ask hard questions.

Chapter 7

Flee Fornication

Flee fornication.
Every sin that a man doeth is without the body;
but he that committeth fornication
sinneth against his own body.

1 Corinthians 6:18

This is one of the clearest pieces of instruction for singles in the Bible. Flee fornication. To flee is to run away often from danger or evil. To flee is to hurry toward a place of security. People try to spiritualize their sexual sins, but most sexual sins are simple products of geography. People wind up fornicating or committing adultery because they were somewhere they shouldn't have been.

The most famous case of sexual indiscretion in the Bible is the case of David and Bathsheba. People talk about David's adultery and the lies and murder that followed to cover it up. They talk about Nathan's confrontation. And they talk about the death of the child that was conceived. There is much talk about David's prayer of repentance in Psalm 51 and the fact that God went on to call David a man after his own heart. But you don't hear much talk about what led up to David's sin.

2 Samuel 11:1

And it came to pass, after the year was expired, at the time when kings go forth to battle, that David sent Joab, and his servants with him, and all Israel; and they destroyed the children of Ammon, and besieged Rabbah. But David tarried still at Jerusalem.

David should have been at battle, but he elected to stay home. Most young people get into trouble between the hours of 3 and 6 pm because they are at home unattended after school. Girls and boys lose their virginity after going off to college. Where you are has a huge bearing on what you do.

Joseph understood that and he applied Paul's philosophy long before Paul wrote it. Maybe he was Paul's inspiration.

Genesis 39:1-13

1 And Joseph was brought down to Egypt; and Potiphar, an officer of Pharaoh, captain of the guard, an Egyptian, bought him of the hands of the Ishmeelites, which had brought him down thither.

2 And the LORD was with Joseph, and he was a prosperous man; and he was in the house of his master the Egyptian.

3 And his master saw that the LORD was with him, and that the LORD made all that he did to prosper in his hand.

4 And Joseph found grace in his sight, and he served him: and he made him overseer over his house, and all that he had he put into his hand.

5 And it came to pass from the time that he had made him overseer in his house, and over all that he had, that the LORD blessed the Egyptian's house for Joseph's sake; and the blessing of the LORD was upon all that he had in the house, and in the field.

6 And he left all that he had in Joseph's hand; and he knew not ought he had, save the bread which he did eat. And Joseph was a goodly person, and well favoured.

7 And it came to pass after these things, that his master's wife cast her eyes upon Joseph; and she said, Lie with me.

8 But he refused, and said unto his master's wife, Behold, my master wotteth not what is with me in the house, and he hath committed all that he hath to my hand;

9 There is none greater in this house than I; neither hath he kept back any thing from me but thee, because thou art his wife: how then can I do this great wickedness, and sin against God?

10 And it came to pass, as she spake to Joseph day by day, that he hearkened not unto her, to lie by her, or to be with her.

11 And it came to pass about this time, that Joseph went into the house to do his business; and there was none of the men of the house there within.

12 And she caught him by his garment, saying, Lie with me: and he left his garment in her hand, and fled, and got him out.

The story of Joseph covers a lot of ground. This dreamer was left in a pit by his jealous brothers and then sold into slavery in lieu of being murdered. He wound up in Potiphar's house as an indentured servant and life got better for a minute.

He was a prosperous man. He was entrusted with the stewardship of his master's house. God blessed the house for Joseph's sake. And then, Potiphar's wife noticed him.

Fornication is not always about sex. People are drawn to power and anointing. They say power is the world's greatest aphrodisiac. The devil will send someone your way to blemish the gift that is in you. If you are not careful, you will damage your destiny because won't control your flesh.

This nameless woman asked Joseph to have sex with her and he refused. But the devil is persistent. He only left Jesus for a season and he is going to keep coming after you, too. Satan wants to break down your resistance. He wants to wear down your defenses. He wants you to forget that your body is not for fornication.

If you continue to refuse, he will wait until you are in a compromised position. Joseph was where he was supposed to be, but he got caught in the house with his master's wife alone. Sometimes you don't have any control over your circumstances, but you always have control over your self.

She grabbed him. She tried to force him. She hoped he would reconsider in the heat of the moment and give in. She hoped that "no" really meant, "yes." But she was wrong. Joseph didn't think. Joseph didn't argue. Joseph didn't pray. Joseph did what anyone who makes it through this life unblemished will have to do sooner or later. He ran.

Joseph left that house and his garments in her hands. Joseph got out of there as fast as he could. He didn't have sex with her. He didn't hug her. He didn't kiss her. He didn't even argue with her. But he suffered the consequence of being alone with her.

Because there were no witnesses, she was able to lie on Joseph. That's why you have to avoid even the appearance of evil. You can control your flesh, but you can't control other people's tongues. Her lies sent him to prison. But his obedience got him out.

You may think that we are overly concerned about fornication, but you need to think again about the consequences. You are a three part being. And everything you do affects every part of you.

Think about your reputation. Think about your health. Think about your freedom. Think about your destiny.

We talked to you earlier about the double standard that all women face. You don't want a whore's reputation. When men start looking for wives, they want to find them pure. Sexually transmitted diseases have become matters of life and death in recent years. Are you willing to risk your life for a moment of pleasure? What if you get pregnant? How will a baby change your plans? And how will your sin affect your conscience? Will opening your legs shut your mouth? Don't play around with this. Flee fornication.

Chapter 8

The Two Become One

And Adam said, This is now bone of my bones,
and flesh of my flesh: she shall be called Woman,
because she was taken out of Man.
Therefore shall a man leave his father and his mother,
and shall cleave unto his wife:
and they shall be one flesh.

Genesis 2:23,24

The most powerful argument against fornication is that two people who engage in sexual intimacy become one flesh. Your favor is tied to that union. Your grace is bound by that bond. Your blessing is wrapped up in that encounter. Sexual intimacy is nothing to play with.

There are people hiding in churches who thought they could get away from their promiscuity. They thought they had overcome their urges, but they just keep failing. It is a real problem and they can't even tell anyone. Now that they are in church, all of their friends are Christians. So they hide. they hide in the congregation and try to pray it away.

If you don't understand your enemy, he will always have victory over you. Your best defense is to flee fornication.

But what do you do after the deed is done? Running will only take care of part of the problem then.

Even if you don't get pregnant. Even if you leave with your health in tact. You are still tainted, damaged even, spiritually. When you joined yourself to another person, both of you opened a door for Satanic activity to enter your lives. There is an enemy emissary occupying your flesh waiting to sabotage any new relationships.

1 Corinthians 6:16

What? know ye not that he which is joined to an harlot is one body? for two, saith he, shall be one flesh.

What may be even more alarming to you is that everytime you add a new partner, you compound the demon activity. Imagine having sex with five, ten, fifteen, men or women prior to getting married. You now have a super human image branded on your spirit, soul, and body. Unless you address that presence, you will find it competing with the true love of your life.

No man or woman can compete with that. You will find yourself constantly unhappy and hopelessly unsatisfied until you deal with it. This is spiritual warfare we're talking about. The devil is your enemy. And the word of God is the only thing he respects.

He hopes that you never find out that your *"body is not for fornication, but for the Lord; and the Lord for the body"* (1 Corinthians 6:13). He hopes you will be so caught up in the temporary pleasure of occasional trysts that you will forget about the eternal consequence and the loss of supernatural power.

We have an adversary. Paul admonished us to *"Be sober, be vigilant; because your adversary the devil, as a roaring lion, walketh about, seeking whom he may devour: Whom resist stedfast in the faith, knowing that the same afflictions are accomplished in your brethren that are in the world"* (1 Peter 5:8,9).

Paul knew what he was talking about. And the devil knows it too. The devil knows that sexual intimacy is intoxicating. People get drunk with love. And while they are swooning their defenses go down. Samson lost his freedom and ultimately his life because he refused to flee fornication. But there is one more thing that you lose when you fornicate. Power.

The greatest power God granted men and women is the power of agreement. When God looked at Adam in the garden and said, *"It is not good that the man should be alone; I will make him an help meet for him."* (Genesis 2:18), God knew that what Adam needed was someone to agree with him.

Agreement gives men and women access to the favor that a man is promised when he finds a wife. Agreement moves heaven and earth. Jesus said, *"if two of you shall agree on earth as touching any thing that they shall ask, it shall be done for them of my Father which is in heaven"* (Matthew 18:19). And the strange thing about agreement, is that it works for sinners and saints. Look at Genesis 11.

Genesis 11:1-6

1 And the whole earth was of one language, and of one speech.

2 And it came to pass, as they journeyed from the east, that they found a plain in the land of Shinar; and they dwelt there.

3 And they said one to another, Go to, let us make brick, and burn them thoroughly. And they had brick for stone, and slime had they for morter.

4 And they said, Go to, let us build us a city and a tower, whose top may reach unto heaven; and let us make us a name, lest we be scattered abroad upon the face of the whole earth.

5 And the LORD came down to see the city and the tower, which the children of men builded.

6 And the LORD said, Behold, the people is one, and they have all one language; and this they begin to do: and now nothing will be restrained from them, which they have imagined to do.

These people were heathens. They were not born again. Jesus had not been born, crucified, or risen. God hadn't even established the nation of Israel yet. But God recognized the power of agreement. And their agreement moved heaven.

The devil wants you to agree against God. He wants you to join the temple of God with a harlot. He wants you to turn that which is holy to that which is inconvenient. Then he has power over you and you have turned your power over to him. Don't do it!

Make a decision today. Decide to preserve that power for eternal purpose. Your body is not for fornication. The quicker you know that the more powerful you will be. King David declared, *"I will praise thee; for I am fearfully and wonderfully made: marvellous are thy works; and that my soul knoweth right well"* (Psalm 139:14). Do you know that about yourself?

You may be alone, but you don't have to be lonely. God had not forgotten you and he certainly has not forsaken you. King David also said, *"The LORD will perfect that which concerneth me: thy mercy, O LORD, endureth for ever: forsake not the works of thine own hands"* (Psalm 138:8). Can you say that? When you do, God will respond. *"I will never leave thee, nor forsake thee"* (Hebrews 13:5).

Make a decision today. Decide not to compromise. Decide to take a stand. Decide you are special. You are the work of God's own hands. Why should you lay down with just anyone? Shouldn't the one you lay down with lift you up? Aren't you worth that much. And shouldn't there be some thought to what the two of you will do with the power that your union will produce?

One flesh. That is what you will become when you enter into sexual intimacy. One flesh. One voice. One destiny.

Isn't that worth waiting for? Isn't that worth considering? Is that something you want to waste on just anyone? No!

Sexual intimacy may well be in your future. And your flesh may have begun to burn. But there is a right way and a wrong way to become one flesh.

Chapter 9
It's Better To Marry

Now concerning the things whereof ye wrote unto me:
It is good for a man not to touch a woman.
Nevertheless, to avoid fornication,
let every man have his own wife,
and let every woman have her own husband.
~ ~
But if they cannot contain, let them marry:
for it is better to marry than to burn.

1 Corinthians 7:1,2 & 9

The second most powerful weapon the Bible prescribes against fornication is marriage. Bottom line--if you are not going to flee fornication, you need to run to marriage. Now that may not sound like the most romantic advice you've ever heard. It may not even sound terribly spiritual. But it is an effective response to a very serious problem. And maybe that is part of the problem. Maybe we have become so caught up in the romance and spirituality of relationships that we have overlooked the practical rules of relationships.

Most people prepare for marriage in the same way their parents and friends prepare for marriage. The meet. They date. They plan a wedding. They say I do. They go on a honeymoon. And they return to the rigors of life.

God's approach to marriage is slightly different. God brought Eve to Adam as his wife--not his girlfriend. There was no dating. There was no courtship. There was no long engagement. There isn't even any evidence of a ceremony or a honeymoon. Eve was divinely designed for Adam. He awakened and saw her and that was that.

Isaac did almost the same thing with Rebekah. This young man, like Adam, didn't get to choose his wife. His father, Abraham, sent a servant to find a wife for his son while Isaac was mourning the death of his mother, Sarah. The servant prayed and God brought Rebekah to him. There was no dating. There was no courtship. There was no engagement. There was no ceremony or honeymoon. The minute Isaac saw Rebekah; he knew she was the one.

Surely there were other women in Abraham's camp. Sarah had handmaidens that Isaac could have just as easily been attracted to. But God brought him a wife. They didn't date. They didn't wait. They went straight into a tent and consummated their union. And they stayed married.

Romance is wonderful. Everybody likes to feel attractive and be pursued. But romances tend to run hot and cold because they are deeply rooted in emotion. Spirituality is great. We all need to be led by the Spirit and let the power of God operate in our lives. But there are good spirits and evil spirits, and some people can't seem to tell one from the other. That's why we need to prepare for marriage by learning the rules. Rules override emotion and help us discern spirits. Even God, who is a Spirit, abides by his word (his rules) so his emotions won't take over.

Malachi 3:6

For I am the LORD, I change not; therefore ye sons of Jacob are not consumed.

Remember those occasions when God grew so angry with the children of Israel that he threatened to destroy them and make a new nation out of Moses? Moses was able to intercede and save the Jews by reminding God of his word and his name. God is not moved by emotion. He obeys his own word and you have to make the same commitment or your flesh will always win its battle with your spirit.

Galatians 5:17

For the flesh lusteth against the Spirit, and the Spirit against the flesh: and these are contrary the one to the other: so that ye cannot do the things that ye would.

Would you be free from fornication? Then either flee or marry. It's that simple.

Marriage is between a man and a woman. Marriage is until death do you part. Marriage is honorable. And the marriage bed is undefiled. Marriage sanctifies relationships.

1 Corinthians 7:13,14

13 And the woman which hath an husband that believeth not, and if he be pleased to dwell with her, let her not leave him.

14 For the unbelieving husband is sanctified by the wife, and the unbelieving wife is sanctified by the husband: else were your children unclean; but now are they holy.

Marrying a Christian won't save an unbeliever from their sins, but marriage will sanctify sex between a believer and an unbeliever and cleanse their children. That is by no means an encouragement for believers to marry unbelievers. The same Paul who wrote concerning the sanctity of marriage also admonished believers not to be unequally yoked with unbelievers. We are simply trying to show you the power of marriage as it pertains to fornication. The marriage bed is undefiled.

Sexual intimacy is a very important part of marriage. If disputes over money are the number one cause of divorce in America, then disputes over sexual intimacy come in a very close second. If you're preparing for marriage, you'd better prepare to have sex. Most marrital trouble arises because people are moved by emotion and they either don't know or won't obey the rules.

1 Corinthians 7:3-5

3 Let the husband render unto the wife due benevolence: and likewise also the wife unto the husband.

4 The wife hath not power of her own body, but the husband: and likewise also the husband hath not power of his own body, but the wife.

5 Defraud ye not one the other, except it be with consent for a time, that ye may give yourselves to fasting and prayer; and come together again, that Satan tempt you not for your incontinency.

The Amplified Bible says it this way...

3 The husband should give to his wife her conjugal rights (goodwill, kindness, and what is due her as his wife), and likewise the wife to her husband.

4 For the wife does not have [exclusive] authority and control over her own body, but the husband [has his rights]; likewise also the husband does not have [exclusive] authority and control over his body, but the wife [has her rights].

5 Do not refuse and deprive and defraud each other [of your due marital rights], except perhaps by mutual consent for a time, so that you may devote yourselves unhindered to prayer. But afterwards resume marital relations, lest Satan tempt you [to sin] through your lack of restraint of sexual desire.

Isn't it strange that people who are single can't seem to keep their hands off of one another but people who are married can go weeks, months, even years, denying each other sex to the point of sleeping in separate bedrooms?

That is nothing but the devil influencing peoples' emotions and attacking them in the realm of the spirit.

When you say, "I do" you agree to a sexual responsibility and you lose a measure of sexual control. You agree to allow your husband or wife to use your body to satisfy their sexual needs as often as they desire. And if you won't, the Bible says you make your spouse vulnerable to satanic attack. The only time the rules entitle you to deny your spouse sex is during a time of prayer and fasting, and you need their permission for that. If we could get married couples to abide by those two rules--pray and fast and have sex every time you're asked--we could save most marriages.

But Paul also said, you don't have to get married. He said his ideas about marriage and sexual intimacy were spoken *"by permission, and not of commandment"* (1 Corinthians 7:6).

Actually, Paul thought it best that people not marry. He didn't want them to fornicate either. Paul wanted Christians to be like him.

There is some question as to whether Paul was married. We know he was a Pharisee and a member of the Sanhedrin. And we know that, according to Jewish law, such men had to be married. We also know that after his conversion, Paul didn't go home again for fourteen to eighteen years.

Maybe he and the Mrs. had an arrangement. Maybe they considered his ministry one long fast. Most people believe he was a widower. We do know that Paul considered it a *"gift of God"* to live without sexual activity. And he knew most people couldn't do it. Which brings us back to Paul's original statement; *"if* [you] *cannot contain, ...marry: for it is better to marry than to burn. "* (1 Corinthians 7:9).

Chapter 10
'Til Death Us Do Part

For the woman which hath an husband
is bound by the law to her husband so long as he liveth;
but if the husband be dead,
she is loosed from the law of her husband.

Romans 7:2

If you're serious about your relationship with God, divorce should be out of the question. Don't discuss it. There are some people who are already married who think it's too late. The thrill is gone. The honeymoon is over. And they are saying to themselves; "I didn't get married to be miserable."

But you have to prepare for days like that now. There will be days when you want to quit. Make a decision now. Get prepared now. Marriage is not all thrills and honeymoons. Marriage demands change. Don't get set in your ways and refuse to adapt. If you are not prepared for some adjustments in your daily routine, you are not prepared to be married.

Some people just can't be married. They have too many quirks that they refuse to change. They have unresolved issues and they are unprepared to have them challenged. Their misery is personal and personal misery has no place in a marriage.

You've got to be happy with yourself before you marry. If you're not, you will soon find yourself competing with the woman at the well in John 4. She had been through five husbands and was shacking up with a man when she met Jesus. The divorces may not have been all her fault, but there were obviously some issues there. You need to be prepared to make the marriage you are in work.

The church has some serious issues to deal with. We're saved but we are still a work in progress. We've got people who are married but don't want to be. We've got singles who want to be married but are unprepared. There is a lot of frustration in the air. Paul's desire *"that all men were even as"* he was sounds pretty good right about now. People who are married to Jesus create a lot less confusion.

Don't carry confusion and dysfunction into your marriage. And please don't marry someone else who is dysfunctional. Such baggage is counterproductive and you are not prepared to shoulder it. What you need is wisdom. You need guidance and direction. You need the word of God. Learn the word at church and apply the word to your life. The word of God makes it clear that divorce is not an option for Christian couples.

Mark 10:1-9

1 And he arose from thence, and cometh into the coasts of Judaea by the farther side of Jordan: and the people resort unto him again; and, as he was wont, he taught them again.

2 And the Pharisees came to him, and asked him, Is it lawful for a man to put away his wife? tempting him.

3 And he answered and said unto them, What did Moses command you?

4 And they said, Moses suffered to write a bill of divorcement, and to put her away.

5 And Jesus answered and said unto them, For the hardness of your heart he wrote you this precept.

6 But from the beginning of the creation God made them male and female.

7 For this cause shall a man leave his father and mother, and cleave to his wife;

8 And they twain shall be one flesh: so then they are no more twain, but one flesh.

9 What therefore God hath joined together, let not man put asunder.

The devil wants you to put your marriage asunder. Satan wants to divide and conquer. That old serpent wants to strip you of your favor and leave you vulnerable to his attacks.

John 10:10

The thief cometh not, but for to steal, and to kill, and to destroy: I am come that they might have life, and that they might have it more abundantly.

You want an abundant life? Get married and stay that way. The average millionaire in America, according to Thomas J. Stanley, author of *The Millionaire Mind*, is a fifty-four year old male who has been married to the same woman for twenty-eight years. Twenty-five percent (or 1 in 4) of millionaires have been married to the same woman for thirty-eight or more years. And ninety-two percent of millionaires are married. Millionaires actually believe that one of the five most important factors that contribute to their success is a supportive spouse.

A supportive spouse means a spouse in agreement. And a spouse in agreement means power from God. God's observation that it was *"not good for the man to be alone"* was all about agreement. God's decision to make Adam an *"help meet"* for him was all about agreement. God's promise to grant *"favor"* to the man who finds a wife is all about agreement. Divorce destroys that favor because divorce is the product of disagreement.

Look at the power of agreement in Genesis 11:1-6. People in agreement moved God and caused him to agree that *"nothing* [would] *be restrained from them, which they* [had] *imagined to do."* Jesus agreed with his Father when he said, *"if two of you shall agree on earth as touching any thing that they shall ask, it shall be done for them of my Father which is in heaven"* (Matthew 18:19). And when Ananias and Sapphira agreed, *"to lie to the Holy Ghost"* it moved the spirit of God to kill them.

Marriage places you in the most powerful position of agreement known to man. Divorce should be out of the question. Divorce neutralizes that place of power. Don't discuss it.

Chapter 11

Peace NOT Confusion

But if the unbelieving depart, let him depart.
A brother or a sister is not under bondage in such cases:
but God hath called us to peace.

1 Corinthians 7:15

As much as we hate divorce, we recognize that there are
some situations where marriages just don't work. That is
why it is so important to prepare before you say I do. Marriage isn't easy under the best circumstances. But for those
who are unprepared it can be overwhelming.

When you add verbal abuse, substance abuse, physical abuse,
and any one of a thousand other dysfunctions to an already
unstable marriage, only the power of God can save it. And
even God recognized man's inability or unwillingness to forgive certain things and offered him and out.

Mark 10:2-5

*2 And the Pharisees came to him, and asked him, Is
it lawful for a man to put away his wife? tempting
him.*

3 And he answered and said unto them, What did Moses command you?

4 And they said, Moses suffered to write a bill of divorcement, and to put her away.

5 And Jesus answered and said unto them, For the hardness of your heart he wrote you this precept.

God doesn't want us to divorce. But God doesn't want our hardness of heart to ruin other peoples' lives either. Paul lays out a few possible separation scenarios in 1 Corinthians 7.

1 Corinthians 7:10-15

10 And unto the married I command, yet not I, but the Lord, Let not the wife depart from her husband:

11 But and if she depart, let her remain unmarried or be reconciled to her husband: and let not the husband put away his wife.

12 But to the rest speak I, not the Lord: If any brother hath a wife that believeth not, and she be pleased to dwell with him, let him not put her away.

13 And the woman which hath an husband that believeth not, and if he be pleased to dwell with her, let her not leave him.

14 For the unbelieving husband is sanctified by the wife, and the unbelieving wife is sanctified by the husband: else were your children unclean; but now are they holy.

15 But if the unbelieving depart, let him depart. A brother or a sister is not under bondage in such cases: but God hath called us to peace.

Paul begins by telling wives not to leave their husbands. But he follows that declaration with a qualifier. If you leave, don't get married again. Plan to reunite, he said. And he gives the same instruction to husbands.

At first, Paul seems to be speaking to Christian couples. But he quickly turns his attention to, shall we say, mixed couples--couples that are unequally yoked. He instructs believers who have unbelieving spouses to remain married as long as the unbeliever wants to stay.

We have seen couples where unbelieving spouses treat their husbands or wives better than some believers. They work hard. They pay their bills. They are thoughtful. They spend time with their children. These are people who don't know Jesus, but in every other way, they are perfect partners. Paul says stay with such partners. Peter agreed.

1 Peter 3:1,2

1 Likewise, ye wives, be in subjection to your own husbands; that, if any obey not the word, they also may without the word be won by the conversation of the wives;

*2 While they behold your chaste conversation cou-
pled with fear.*

Obey your husbands, Peter says, even if they don't obey the
word. Wow! That doesn't mean follow them into sin. It
simply means that most of marriage is not spiritual. Marriage is cooking dinner and changing sheets. Marriage is
changing diapers and making love. Marriage is making
plans and seeing them through. If your unsaved husband
says, "fix me some eggs," don't argue with him and call him
a sinner. Fix the man some eggs. And if your atheist wife
needs you to pick up the kids after school don't talk to her
about how she's going to get left behind if she doesn't know
Jesus, just pick up the kids. Bottom line--if they are pleased
to dwell with you, you be pleased too.

Your righteousness in Christ Jesus carries a lot more weight
than you think. You don't have to beat your spouse over the
head with the Bible. Paul said, *"the unbelieving husband is
sanctified by the wife, and the unbelieving wife is sanctified
by the husband."* Sanctified means set apart. And that sanc-
tification has a profound impact on your children.

If, however, your unbelieving spouse decides to act out his
sinful nature and skips out on you, God does not require you
to bemoan the loss in solitude. No. God says move on. Get
a life. Remarry if you like. Paul said, *"A brother or a sister
is not under bondage in such cases: but God hath called us
to peace."*

Peace. Isn't that what we are all after in our marriages? But peace doesn't just happen. You have to prepare for peace. You have to plan for peace. You may actually have to fight for peace in your family. God does.

Romans 16:20

And the God of peace shall bruise Satan under your feet shortly. The grace of our Lord Jesus Christ be with you. Amen.

Your fight should be with the devil. *"For we wrestle not against flesh and blood, but against principalities, against powers, against the rulers of the darkness of this world, against spiritual wickedness in high places"* (Ephesians 6:12). But when the fighting turns on you physically, call the law. Don't call the pastor for prayer. Call the police.

Ladies, especially, never let anyone abuse you physically. The first time any man hits you should be the last time. Call the police and leave. Actually, leave first and then call the police.

Domestic violence is a huge problem all over the world. The Centers for Disease Control cites 'unintentional injuries' as the #6 cause of death among American women. Intimate Partner Violence (IPV) is a major cause of 'unintentional injuries.' Expect the best from your husband or wife, but you need to be prepared for the worst.

If you are not married yet, don't marry an unbeliever. If you are already married to an unbeliever and all is well, don't destroy your marriage trying to convert your spouse. Live upright before your spouse and love them and let the Spirit of God lead them to Jesus. If the unbelieving spouse wants to dwell with you, don't drive them away. If the unbelieving spouse chooses to depart, let them depart. Get a life. Remarry. Move on. Remember: God has called us to peace. And never allow yourself to be abused. Get out and call the law.

Finally. You should never initiate separation or divorce. If you are married, prepare to stay married. Find a way to make your marriage work. If you need a break for a season, take a break. Separate. Stay single. And do all you can to reunite. And never forget: *"A brother or a sister is [never] under bondage...God hath called us to peace."*

Chapter 12

Too Late

The woman answered and said, I have no husband. Jesus said unto her, Thou hast well said, I have no husband: For thou hast had five husbands; and he whom thou now hast is not thy husband: in that saidst thou truly.

John 4:17,18

As we said earlier, there are married people who believe that it is too late for their marriages to get any better. But there are single people who believe that they are past the point of desirability, also. Some of them they think they are too old. Others believe they have been through too many relationships. Many are worried that they are past childbearing age. As many others fear they have too many children with too many partners. And all of them think it is too late for them to be happily married.

For every one of these examples, we can show you people who were in the same situation and are now in great marriages. They simply prepared for marriage from where they were. If you are still alive, it's not too late. Solomon said, *"...to him that is joined to all the living there is hope: for a living dog is better than a dead lion"* (Ecclesiastes 9:4).

Every day you live you are getting older. The only alternative to that is death. But people still fight aging, and they don't want to die. As we reach benchmark birthdays, people even start to make declarations about us. "You're over the hill." "You're no spring chicken any more." If you haven't accomplished certain things (like getting married and having children) by a particular age, people really start talking. "She's an old maid." "He's washed up." "The old biological clock is ticking. Tick Tock. Tick Tock."

You can't let people's wagging tongues determine your destiny. Remember; *"ye were sometimes darkness, but now are ye light in the Lord: walk as children of light"* (Ephesians 5:8). We are Christians. *"We walk by faith and not by sight"* (2 Corinthians 5:7). Jesus is Alpha and Omega, the beginning and the ending and he knew your end from the beginning. It doesn't matter what they think. God says, *"... I know the thoughts that I think toward you, saith the LORD, thoughts of peace, and not of evil, to give you an expected end"* (Jeremiah 29:11). Who are you going to agree with, the backbiters or God?

Enjoy living holy and embrace your salvation while you are single. Be happy to be saved. And whatever you do, don't grow *"weary in well doing"* (Galatians 6:9). You love God. And you know that the love of God is *"that we keep his commandments: and his commandments are not grievous"* (1 John 5:3). So keep on loving God.

Invite those wagging tongues to church. Show them that it is better to live holy alone than to share a bed and a future with the devil. Show them that you are healthier and wealthier because you have been obedient and patient. Let them see that *"The righteous is more excellent than his neighbour"* (Proverbs 12:26). And never let the way of the wicked seduce you.

We were so fortunate. We have three boys and one daughter. They all work with us in the ministry. Our daughter made a decision early on to serve the Lord. People ask us, "What did you do?" The truth is, we can't point to any one thing. We tried to be good examples before her, but she made the decision to serve the Lord herself.

Many of us old folks wish we could go back and change some of our choices. Most of us wish we had chosen to serve the Lord before we chose our spouses. But yesterday is gone and the damage is done. This is the day that the Lord has made. And you have to decide today to receive God's expected end for your life.

You have to desire it. And you have to aspire to it. You can't just want what God has for you. You need a plan. *"For a dream cometh through the multitude of business; and a fool's voice is known by multitude of words"* (Ecclesiastes 5:3).

First of all, don't sit around and wait for some prince to come along and change your life. You plan for your future. Boaz is not looking for a lazy needy person. Boaz noticed Ruth because she was taking charge of her own destiny. She was industrious. She was focused. She was prepared. She was also a widow taking care of her widowed mother-in-law. But that didn't stop her. Ruth maintained her chastity and got busy.

You should maintain your chastity while you are single, too. And if you are not sexually active, you can't get pregnant. But that's about the full extent of your limitations. You can earn a living. You can manage your own money. You can give. You can save. You can invest. You can build a home. You can even run a business.

Mary Kay Ash, for example, started the business bears her name as a divorcee with three children. She, like many women, got married at an early age but the marriage didn't last. Once divorced, she went to work and found that her talent was no match for sexism in corporate America. So, she retired at 45 and used the manuscript for an intended book as a business plan. She and her son started Mary Kay cosmetics with $5,000 and took the high road to success--in a pink Cadillac.

She never married again, but she helped thousands of women to succeed while placing "God first, family second, and business third."

What is your plan for your future? Is God first? Or are you so desperate to have a family that you are willing to do anything to get one? Get your priorities straight and wait on the Lord. It's not too late.

We said it earlier, but it bears saying again; you may have made some bad choices in the past, but you can begin now to prepare. You can make yourself marketable. We know that word sounds a bit less than "spiritual" but it is critical that you understand that the Boaz's of this world are shopping. Each one is looking for his Ruth. And he wants Ruth to be prepared.

Remember: You need to be prepared spiritually, financially, emotionally, physically, and domestically.

Please, don't even consider marrying someone who is not born again. For those of you who are mature in the Lord, you want your spouse to be Spirit-filled and Spirit-led. You should never marry someone who is not as excited about going to church as you are. And it is best that husbands and wives go to the same church. Finally, you both need to be in the word and doers of the word. It is the word of God that will best prepare you for marriage.

Don't forget: Marriages need finances to survive. You cannot live on love alone. One of the greatest causes of divorce in America is disputes over money, usually the lack of it. Men, you need a job, a sustainable source of income, before you get married. Men and women need to do their very best to get out of debt before they get married. Debt creates a burden that is difficult to bear for any marriage. If you have debts, you should make your future spouse aware of them going into the marriage. And you both need to be tithers.

You are going to need somewhere to live. The married man is instructed to *"leave his father and his mother, and shall cleave unto his wife"* (Genesis 2:24). If you're going to get married, you're going to need a house. Jesus said, *"I go to prepare a place for you"* (John 14:2). No respectable Jewish man can get married until his father approves of the accommodations he has prepared for his bride.

You are going to need viable transportation. How will you get to work? How will you get to church? How will your kids get to school? These are all things you must consider before you get married.

Marriage should never be used as an opiate to dull the pain of your personal self-esteem problems. Love does not satisfy itself at the expense of others. Love gives. *"For God so loved the world, he gave..."* (John 3:16). It is unfair to expect someone else to shoulder the burden of your low self-esteem. No man or woman can make you "feel good" about yourself forever.

The intimacy of marriage will expose all your inhibitions. If you are not ready to have those flaws revealed, you are not ready to be married. We will talk more about this when we get to domestic issues, but you have to ask yourself: "How can I hang on to my hang-ups if my body is not my own?"

If you have been married before or in multiple relationships, you must be sure you have dealt with all your unresolved issues. It is not fair to hold your current spouse hostage to the faults of your ex. It's not too late for you to get married, but you have to deal with your issues before you get married.

Love is grand, but marriage can get real practical. Are you ready to keep a clean house? Are you prepared for consistent sexual intimacy? Can you handle the challenge of paying bills, even ones you didn't make? Can you manage a household, and a life that is filled with other people? And what will you do when it's time to raise children?

All of these issues will be affected by your understanding of the individual roles & expectations each of you bring to the marriage. Should the man be the sole breadwinner? Should the wife be the primary care giver? Who has the last word in major decisions? These are all questions that both of you must have compatible answers to. Use your wait time to make your choices because after the wedding it will be too late.

Pastors Frank & JoeNell Summerfield

Chapter 13
Faith Comes By Hearing

So then faith cometh by hearing,
and hearing by the word of God.

Romans 10:17

As we bring this book to a close, we want to draw your attention, once again, to the word of God. The best preparation anyone can make for marriage is to become firmly rooted in the word. You may learn the word at church, but you have to do the word every day. Don't deceive yourself into believing that you've got it just because you hear it taught. You must be a doer of the word or you will never be prepared for anything, especially marriage.

Hebrews 11:3

Through faith we understand that the worlds were
framed by the word of God, so that things which are
seen were not made of things which do appear.

God made everything by his word. If he didn't make it then it just wasn't made. God made your husband. God made your wife. He has known you from before the foundation of the world and he knows exactly whom you need. Learn his word and you will discover his will for your life.

John 1:1-3

1 In the beginning was the Word, and the Word was with God, and the Word was God.

2 The same was in the beginning with God.

3 All things were made by him; and without him was not any thing made that was made.

Hearing and doing the word of God will help you to develop discretion and intensify your discernment. In other words, it will help you to know good folks from bad ones. Have you ever noticed, maybe even about yourself, that some people always seem to choose the wrong people? They have no discernment because they are measuring people by the wrong standards. When you know the word, you elevate your standard to God's standard and God knows how to pick 'em.

It is sad to watch people do well for years only to lose their minds over a man or a woman. Lust seems to make them forget everything they know. It must be lust because love does not behave itself unseemly and unseemly behavior is what most of these relationships are about.

Peter and Paul noticed that people forget too. That's why they kept reminding the churches of the word. That's why we are determined to remind you, too.

Hebrews 5:12-14

12 For when for the time ye ought to be teachers, ye

have need that one teach you again which be the first principles of the oracles of God; and are become such as have need of milk, and not of strong meat.

13 For every one that useth milk is unskilful in the word of righteousness: for he is a babe.

14 But strong meat belongeth to them that are of full age, even those who by reason of use have their senses exercised to discern both good and evil.

2 Peter 1:12

Wherefore I will not be negligent to put you always in remembrance of these things, though ye know them, and be established in the present truth.

Once you are established in the truth (Jesus / the living word) you will be able to spot a lie and/or a liar. Get in the word. Learn the word. Do the word. The word of God will prepare you to choose or be chosen. The word will also steer you away from the wrong choices. Knowing and doing the word of God may actually even save your life.

Proverbs 2:11-17

11 Discretion shall preserve thee, understanding shall keep thee:

12 To deliver thee from the way of the evil man, from the man that speaketh froward things;

13 Who leave the paths of uprightness, to walk in the ways of darkness;

14 Who rejoice to do evil, and delight in the frowardness of the wicked;

15 Whose ways are crooked, and they froward in their paths:

16 To deliver thee from the strange woman, even from the stranger which flattereth with her words;

17 Which forsaketh the guide of her youth, and forgetteth the covenant of her God.

These are the kinds of people many of you have been choosing. You didn't know any better before you were saved, because you didn't know the word. But now you can be on the look out. And God will protect you too. Paul actually asked the saints at Thessalonica to pray that God would keep him away from such people.

2 Thessalonians 3:1,2

1 Finally, brethren, pray for us, that the word of the Lord may have free course, and be glorified, even as it is with you:

2 And that we may be delivered from unreasonable and wicked men: for all men have not faith.

Remember: *"faith cometh by hearing, and hearing by the word of God"* (Romans 10:17). If you want a faith-filled spouse, you had better choose a word-filled spouse. How will you know the difference if you are not filled with the word yourself?

Psalm 127:1

Except the LORD build the house, they labour in vain that build it: except the LORD keep the city, the watchman waketh but in vain. It is vain for you to rise up early, to sit up late, to eat the bread of sorrows: for so he giveth his beloved sleep.

This is your life and legacy we are talking about. This is the mark you will make on the world. Your children will be born of these choices. And your children will probably make their choices based on the example you set before them. Don't spend a lifetime and gamble your future on anything but the word.

Your knowledge of the word will affect your finances, too. Don't forget: Marriages need money. It is God that gives us *"the power to get wealth"* (Deuteronomy 8:18). Your health and your prosperity are tied to the word that you know and do. (3 John 2) As you prepare for marriage, you must prepare financially. And you will only be prepared if you know the word.

Proverbs 24:3,4

3 Through wisdom is an house builded; and by under-

standing it is established:

*4 And by knowledge shall the chambers be filled with
all precious and pleasant riches.*

Wisdom and understanding start with what you hear. It's
that simple. When Adam and Eve sinned in the garden, God
wanted to know who told them they were naked. God knew,
and you should know that your life is impacted by whom you
listen to and what they tell you. Faith comes by hearing.

Who you marry is one of the most important choices you
will ever make. There are almost seven billion people on
this planet and most of them are not for you. Do you want to
trust your future and your family to trial and error? Wouldn't
you rather have the wisdom of God working for you when
you make this choice? Get in the word. Learn the word. Do
the word. The word of God will prepare you to choose or
be chosen.

Chapter 14

Are You Prepared?

For which of you, intending to build a tower,
sitteth not down first, and counteth the cost,
whether he have sufficient to finish it?
Lest haply, after he hath laid the foundation,
and is not able to finish it,
all that behold it begin to mock him,
Saying, This man began to build,
and was not able to finish.

Luke 14:28-30

By now we hope you will agree that there is no question that you need to prepare before you say, "I do." So the only question that remains to be answered is:

Are you prepared?

Let's spend the next few minutes reviewing the key areas where preparation is critical and create a checklist that will help you to assess your readiness to enter into a beautiful bond that will last a lifetime.

Remember: you need to be prepared spiritually, financially, emotionally, physically, and domestically.

Are You Prepared Spiritually

Read (2 Corinthians 6:14)

1. Is your intended born again?
2. Is your intended Spirit-filled and does their lifestyle indicate that they are Spirit-led?
3. Do you believe the person you are about to marry is as excited about going to church as you are?
4. Have you discussed whether you will both go to the same church?
5. Are you both in the word and doers of the word?

It is the word of God that will best prepare you for marriage.

Are You Prepared Financially

Read 1 Timothy 5:8

1. Is one of you gainfully employed and earning enough income to sustain your family?
2. Are both of you tithers?
3. Do either or both of you bring debt to the marriage?
4. Do you have any savings or investments?
5. Are you adequately insured to cover any health issues, loss of employment, and or death?
6. Do you have somewhere to live?
7. Do you have viable transportation?

123 6

Are You Prepared Emotionally

Read Philippians 4:6-8 & Isaiah 26:3

1. Have you been married before?
2. Have you addressed any and all issues that may have a bearing on your new relationship?
3. Does your intended know about any fears or insecurities you may have relative to marriage?
4. Are you trusting God to meet your emotional needs, or are you looking for your spouse to do that?
5. Have you both been through marriage counseling?

Are You Prepared Domestically

Read Titus 2:1-8

1. Are you ready to keep a clean house?
2. Are you prepared for consistent sexual intimacy?
3. Can you handle the challenge of paying bills, even ones you didn't make?
4. Can you manage a household, and a life that is filled with other people?
5. What will you do when it's time to raise children?
6. Should the man be the sole breadwinner?
7. Should the wife be the primary care giver?
8. Who has the last word in major decisions?

Pastors Frank & JoeNell Summerfield

About The Authors

Dr. Frank Summerfield, Ph D

Dr. Frank Summerfield is the founder and Pastor of Word of God Fellowship in Raleigh, NC. Word of God Fellowship is an active ministry with outreach through TV, a Day Care Center serving 170 children, and a Christian Academy for grades K-12 serving more than 200 children.

Dr. Summerfield has a B.A. in Health & Physical Education from Kansas Wesleyan University Salina, Kansas, a M.A. in Health Education from Montclair State University, and a Doctorate of Divinity Degree from Saint Thomas Christian College of Jacksonville, Florida.

The Summerfields have enjoyed more than 33 years of marriage. Their four children, Music Minister Frank Jr., Executive Coordinator Mitchell, Human Resource/Personnel Director Valisha, and Joshua are actively involved and supportive of the ministry. Dr. Summerfield travels extensively, ministering to the needs of the Body of Christ. He is currently seen nationally and internationally on The Word Network as well as a host of local and regional network channels.

Dr. Summerfield's authored books include: *Knowing our Delegated Authority, God's Formula for Personal Success and Prosperity, The Supernatural Power of Your Vision, All*

You Need is a Good Brain Washing, How to Make Your Marriage Produce Fruit, and *How to Turn Your Prison Into Your Prosperity.*

Mrs. JoeNell Summerfield

Co-Pastor JoeNell Summerfield is the wife of Bishop Frank Summerfield. Together they Pastor Word of God Fellowship Church in Raleigh, NC. They currently minister to millions on The Word Network as well as other local and regional Network channels. They have an active ministry with outreach through a Day care Center and a Christian Academy for grades K-12.

With over 33 years of marriage she is a great asset to her husband. She co-authors the book, How to Make Your Marriage Produce Fruit.

Mrs. Summerfield is the mother of four very supportive children, Music Minister Elder Frank Jr., Elder Mitchell, Elder Valisha, and Joshua all who work in the ministry.

Her method of teaching the Word of God is a down to earth and practical approach of demonstrating to others how to please God and be REAL.